A Closer Look

Michael A. Godfrey

A CLOSER LOOK

SIERRA CLUB BOOKS   SAN FRANCISCO   *1975*

The Sierra Club, founded in 1892 by John Muir, has devoted itself to the study and protection of the nation's scenic and ecological resources—mountains, wetlands, woodlands, wild shores and rivers. All Club publications are part of the nonprofit effort the Club carries on as a public trust. There are some 50 chapters coast to coast, in Canada, Hawaii and Alaska. Participation is invited in the Club's program to enjoy and preserve wilderness everywhere. Address: 1050 Mills Tower, San Francisco, California 94104.

Library of Congress Cataloging in Publication Data

Godfrey, Michael A   1940-
    A closer look.

    1. Natural history.   2. Urban fauna.   I. Title.
QH45.5.G6   574.909'73'2   75-8961
ISBN 0-87156-143-3

Book design by Anita Walker Scott.

Production by Charlsen + Johansen & Others.

Printed in the United States of America.

Contents

List of Illustrations   vii

Acknowledgments   ix

1/LIFE ON A BULLTHISTLE   3

2/THE STREAM   14

3/SPRING EPHEMERALS   42

4/PLANT SUCCESSION   59

5/DEADWOOD   75

6/WINTER BIRDS   92

7/THE COURTSHIP OF THE GRASSES   110

8/CATERPILLARS—IN THEIR OWN RIGHT   121

9/THE ECOSYSTEM IN MY HOUSE   133

Selected Index   145

List of Illustrations

1   LIFE ON A BULLTHISTLE

     Five-lined skink on thistle   5
     Painted lady on thistle   9
     Bumblebee moth and skipper around thistle   11
     Robber-fly and prey   12

2   THE STREAM

     Water strider   19
     Salamander with eggs   23
     Stonefly naiad   26
     Caddisfly net and caddis larva   28
     Crawfish and dace   35
     Cardinal flower and hummingbird   36
     Raccoon dining on frog legs   41

3   SPRING EPHEMERALS

     Trout lily growing through melting snow   49
     Toothwort and trout lily at base of oak tree   51
     Dutchman's breeches   55
     Toothwort with syrphid fly   57

4   PLANT SUCCESSION

     Red admiral on asters   67
     Oak and hickory canopy   70

Sub-dominant hardwoods: dogwood, redbud and sourwood   71
Indian pipes   73
Blueberries and viburnums   73

5   DEADWOOD

Young horned owls in dead poplar   77
Fungi and slime molds on deadwood   84
Wood-eating Passalus larva   86
Millipede   89
Killer fungus, *Cordiceps militaria*   90
Narrow-mouthed toad   91

6   WINTER BIRDS

Brown creeper   95
Evening grosbeak   97
Cardinals   106

7   THE COURTSHIP OF THE GRASSES

Linyphiid spider   113
Orchard grass in full flower   115
Gamma grass   118
Syrphid fly on dallis grass flower   120

8   CATERPILLARS—IN THEIR OWN RIGHT

Setiferous tubercles of polyphemus moth larva (caterpillar)   124
Rough green snake and caterpillar on strawberry bush   125
Paper wasp attacking tent caterpillar   126
Saddleback caterpillar and larva   127
Royal walnut caterpillar   128
Sawfly larva   129
Geometrid caterpillar on safety line   130

9   THE ECOSYSTEM IN MY HOUSE

Black rat snake and mouse   135
Praying mantis   137
Wolf spider, egg clutch and young spiders   139
Brown bat   141
Carolina wren feeding young   142

Acknowledgments

MY THANKS to Dr. Lytton Musselman of the Biology Department of Old Dominion University for his technical review of the chapter on grasses, to Drs. C. Richie Bell and William J. Koch of the University of North Carolina Botany Department for their criticisms of the chapters on plant succession and wood decay respectively and to Dr. Elizabeth A. McMahan of the UNC Zoology Department for her help with the insects which appear in this book. Dr. Michael A. Bleyman of the UNC Zoology Department has my gratitude for his careful and comforting general technical review of the text. Thanks are also due to Dr. Clifford R. Parks and Albert E. Radford of the UNC Botany Department for their suggestions on plant ephemeralism and to Stanley Alford for his help with the reptiles. My special thanks to Rachel Edmonson for her help in preparing the text.

Beyond these specific contributions, the friends mentioned above and many others have helped me over the years more than I can say to see the life processes around me. I could never repay them.

M. G.

A Closer Look

1 / *Life on a Bullthistle*

HOME. Early morning, late April. The day is clear. At dawn there was frost, but soon the sun smiled and the crystals quickly melted. Winter, a wraith of misted frost, hovered briefly above the pasture, then steamed away.

The grass is dry now. I top a little crest and see the bluejay screaming from a sweet gum at wood's edge. The bird strains to shriek its rage at the grasslands. The bluejay is a loudmouth given to posturing and pronouncements, but this is no ordinary sass. It is a cry of frustration—a directly translatable stream of four-letter words.

My ankle touches the bullthistle. It smarts. I add a curt expletive to the bluejay's sulfurous invective, resisting an impulse to kick the plant. Glaring at the pile of needle-tipped green tongues, I see the skink, its head cocked up at me from the foliage.

The outraged bluejay. An unphilosophical human rubbing his ankle. A smug skink. A bullthistle.

My anger mellows to discomfort, then dissolves into curiosity. I retreat two paces and, carefully avoiding another bullthistle, sit down to watch.

The bullthistle, a winter annual, is still a flattened rosette of bristly foliage waiting for this moment's warmth to start the growth that will send it towering beyond a tall man's reach. The skink basks and dozes amid a forest of pines, its body temperature, appetite and enthusiasm for life rising with the sun, with the ecliptic. From time to time the little lizard with the azure tail disappears beneath the spiked foliage to poke its head up elsewhere, in search of the gaily colored crickets which share this protective solarium. The crickets, for their defense, have only to jump to the thickly spiked center of the plant.

The skink pounces, but retreats quickly; foiled by the dense pincushion of the plant's fresh growth, it retires down the center channel of an older leaf where it comfortably fits between the rows of upturned spines. In the little reptile's supposedly expressionless eye, I believe I see a glint of annoyance. Its throat pulses rhythmically, for all I know a soundless skink language echoing the bluejay's ranting. "What the hell? I made an everyday pass at legitimate prey, and this plant stuck me!"

As I watch the game of hide-and-seek at shoelace height, it is clear that the bullthistle has brought the skink and cricket together. The plant completely shelters both creatures from outside attack. Directly or indirectly, it provides both with food. To me and to the bluejay, the thistle is pure pain. But to the cricket and skink it is high habitat, provided they respect the house rules.

That is the relationship; plant harbors reptile and insect, frustrates bird and man. The interplay is simple now. None of the participants has really shaken off the numbness of winter. But it looks pregnant, as if it might be one of those life relationships which expands exponentially with the energy it absorbs. No, not linear; the energy is not used just once; it is captured, held, yielded, used and reused a dozen times over. And all the while more energy continues to pour in from the sun.

The thistle is special because it is common. And accessible. It is an ordinary weed of the open spaces over temperate North America. We need take no safari to distant savannahs to find it. Yet on its own scale, a thistle community is just as magnificent as an African fellowship of ungulates, hunting cats and scavengers. And perhaps because of its availability, the plant is more important to us. The thistle pokes a chink in the patina of plastic consumerism isolating us from our beginnings, from the natural systems that presently sustain us. A hundred dozen other expressions of nature then immediately pry at the thistle's crack. This book observes several phenomena chosen from the nearly infinite interplay of life around us; chosen because in my wanderings near

4

home I stumbled over them often enough that they, perhaps a little more than others, gently coalesced to make nature a compelling thing for me.

That sounds somehow didactic—as if I had found a unified way

A five-lined skink basks in the new foliage of a growing thistle.

5

of seeing life's flow which I now insist on sharing with you. Of course it isn't so. I do not have a special understanding of the biotic ferment to urge upon you. I believe that life in that sense is unknowable. Each discovery reveals deeper ignorance. The horizon of understanding always recedes, largely because of relationships between organisms. The discovery of one relationship implies the existence of others. And the questions you must ask to know those others hint at others still.

It may be strange but I do not find this discouraging. I might if I were a scientist trying to learn more and more about less and less, but I am only a gawking layman delighted at having discovered the obvious. It is enough for me to try to see a few of the relationships around me, to speculate on the vast mysteries they imply. I will know only a little, if I am lucky, about the kinship between cricket and skink. But I can see that they are related, through the bullthistle, to one another and to countless other lives. That perspective lends meaning to the beauty I see, and to my own life.

It is June now. Sun Devils shimmer over the pasture's riot of rank growth. The horse has munched selective blotches and paths between the thistles, enjoying their cool prickle against his flank. The plant's upturned arms plead for the surging sunlight and spread to catch it. An inflorescence swells at the tip of each branch. Some already show a pink tuft. From a few yards away, the thistles resemble giant candelabra, pink flame throbbing at the tips of yellow-green candles of foliage.

The sun is directly overhead; the horse firmly straddles his shadow. The thistle community races about the plant in restless adolescence. Your first close observations at this stage leave a sense of runaway growth and confusion. The thistle is a megalopolis of disorganized prosperity, crime in the streets, indiscriminate public fornication.

That impression is, of course, a transference of human communal ills to a much more refined society. Here the rules are crystal clear, the laws ineluctable. The organization falls short of bureaucracy only in that there is no waste. You are drawn into intimate communication with this community by that wonderful human weakness which seeks order. Or seeks at least

6

to appreciate it. But the frenzied activity resolves itself into a series of purposeful individual missions. What you first saw as chaos you now see instinctively as an ordered government.

A treehopper is on fixed station in the exact center of a thistle leaf. A jagged ridge runs the length of the hopper's back obscuring its outline. Its tubular mouth parts pierce the midvein to tap the riches of the thistle's plumbing. Hour after hour the treehopper stands anchored to this spot, placidly sipping the plant's juices. At intervals this tiny relative of the aphids and cicadas exudes a droplet of "honeydew" waste very high in sugar content. I have seen two species of ants "farming" these treehoppers, stroking them with their antennae to appropriate honeydew. In return, the ants violently defend the hoppers against all intruders, including meddlesome human fingers. Flies dab the honeydew off leaf surfaces beneath the treehoppers. Snails move ponderously over the foliage on highways of mucus to recover the sweetness. In the heat of the summer, you see April's promise of complexity begin to unfold with this humble little homopteran taking sugar from the thistle's bloodstream and with it feeding four other creatures. Or is it a multitude?

It is hard to make a case for the thistle's foliage sustaining a great population of grazing animals and insects; most would choose friendlier fodder. Yet a few stalwarts are possessed of a very special gustatory determination. You frequently notice a hole chewed in a thistle leaf. I have seen something that looks like a clickbeetle mouthing the edges of such an opening. I have seen a snail, leaving a track thinner than the surrounding foliage, apparently eating an upper layer of leaf tissue. And once, only once, I saw a grasshopper munch a great gap in the main stalk. More frequently I see grasshoppers eating the floral parts.

There is always an assortment of thistle dwellers whose function and food source are unclear. I am uncertain, for example, whether to include the bulk of crickets, beetles, grasshoppers and caterpillars in the category which feeds directly on the plant. But every summer I find some creature, that I had assumed was there only to gain protection, eagerly gobbling the foliage.

Then there are the pollinators. It is this category of visitor which sets the bullthistle apart as a plant to ponder. Many, per-

7

The painted lady is a member of the genus Vanessa, *commonly called the thistle butterflies.*

haps most, flowering plants attract a very limited and loyal group of pollinators. Some can be pollinated only by a single species of insect or bird. But the bullthistle is thoroughly promiscuous. It attracts a diverse swarm of pollen-bearers to assist at its nuptials. I cannot describe the intense beauty of a thistle in flower, attended by the kaleidoscopic colors of its regiment of pollinators.

Atop each of the urn-shaped seed cases, the bullthistle bears a profusion of tiny pink flowers in a tight cluster. As these flowers develop, they are visited by waves of bugs, bees, moths, flies, butterflies and hummingbirds. The plant flowers at its branch tips as it grows, so that there are usually several of the pink flashes at their prime on each thistle throughout the summer. Without fail, any time of the day or night, there are insects at work on these blossoms. There are tiny bugs and beetles which probably complete their life cycle moving amid the forest of florets, gleaning wasted pollen grains and playing hide-and-seek with prospective mates. And larger flying insects, including the six-inch tiger swallowtail, labor over the face of the inflorescence, tediously tapping the tiny pools of nectar at the bottom of each floret.

Butterflies provide some of the greatest rewards of bullthistle-watching. A concert of colors, especially with backlighting from a low sun, plays between the dancing wings and the blazing floral torches. Or they may clash resoundingly; pink is a tough color to complement. The monarchs' orange and the hairstreak's blue-gray fail magnificently. The sulfurs and the dark swallowtails triumph in brilliance. About the painted lady I am undecided. Her delicate scallops of brown and orange seem somehow out of place against the hot pinks, but her chromatic tease is one we must accept: the group to which she belongs is so strangely associated with these flowers that its members are called simply the "thistle butterflies."

The list of flying insects which visit thistle flowers is almost as boring to recite as it is fascinating to watch. (It might be easier to eliminate the few who seem to abstain.) Bees and diurnal moths are very prominent. Bumblebees march in methodical circles over the floral heads, stumbling over relatives as small as the pollen baskets on the bumblebees' legs. With a watch glass,

8

you can see bees that might pass for fruit flies save for the pin-heads of pollen they have collected. You can become so engrossed in watching the bumblebee traffic that you hardly notice the imposter in their midst. The bumblebee moth, the bumblebee's mimic, hovers atop the flowers on transparent wings, probing with a tongue the length of its body. Most moths escape the attention of birds by feeding at night. The bumblebee moth masquerades in broad daylight in the costume of a bee which enjoys a broad avian respect. I have known the joy, so help me, of seeing both the bumblebee and its more graceful mimic together at a thistle flower. Naturally, I fumbled with the camera and missed the picture. But that's all right. I can close my eyes and see them anytime I want to.

Be careful on your first visit to any thistle patch. A sobering experience could overtake you. Steel yourself if you hear in the background a rattling twitter that sounds like a kingfisher arguing with a mouse. A few seconds later you might be accosted by a hummingbird who will arrive point-blank in front of your face, to hover there blocking your way and demanding your credentials. To underscore its point, this imperious mite then makes a few symbolic visits to the thistle flowers nearest you. *These are his thistle flowers.* If you are so ill-mannered as to stay, the humming bird usually quits the field with a chittering swoop. The encounter leaves you chuckling nervously to yourself. Aside from these compulsive territorial displays, hummingbirds may be drawn to the flower's sweetness. Their main interest, however, is probably protein in the form of tiny insects hiding in the canyons between the florets.

By the presence of these flying jewels alone, we may deem the thistle's beauty consummate. But it is by a community's predators that we sense its strength and depth. A predator needs a stable food supply; a prey population from which to trim the excess numbers, leaving a breeding stock to produce a sustained yield. In return, predators provide for their prey and actuarial service favoring the removal of the sick, the inept and those with hindering mutations. Predation is the grindstone against which is shaped the stuff of evolution. It keeps prey communities healthy in the present, genetically fit for the future. I know of no setting in which this critical process is more visible than on a bullthistle community.

On the thistle we find a platoon of predators taking advantage of the plant's population of feeders, breeders and pollinators.

A bumblebee moth hovers opposite a skipper as both take nectar from a thistle inflorescence.

Rising from its protected hunting perch, a robber-fly hawks small flying insects.

The mind begins to boggle as we see several levels of predation at work together. Minor predators become the prey of intermediate hunters who ultimately yield their substance to such major marauders as the mantis and the skink. A tiny species of crab-spider often waits at the narrow waist of the floral head to nab unwary (and correspondingly small) pollinators, often snaring small bees and syrphid flies. And I have seen this same crab-spider adjust its position—regrettable timing for a hunter who usually waits motionless—and catch the eye of a jumping spider. It was soon being devoured by the salticid. On another occasion I saw an assassin bug probing the abdomen of a similar salticid. Later I saw a mantis, a male I think, plucking and munching assassin bugs one by one from a family group in the thistle foliage. And we may presume that the male mantis eventually filled the gullet of its mate.

This particular chain could easily have included a big robber fly snatching a smaller species of robber fly, as the latter rose from its protected hunting perch to hawk a winged pollinator. And the big robber fly could easily fall prey to the even bigger writing spider, whose web spans half the thistle's leeward side to snare flying and leaping insects.

September. After a summer's thistle-watching, you have put together the rudiments of your personal *Who's Who* in thistle society. You might well be moved to recognize the mantis as the community's chief executioner. The title fits, less because of the adroit snatching of victims from their supposed sanctuary than for the mantis's relationship with the thistle itself. Where I live,

12

in the Piedmont region of North Carolina, I find that bullthistles, as often as not, have a resident mantis slowly stalking the greenery to strike with dazzling speed when its prey is at last within reach. The body colors I have seen on the Carolina mantis *always* match the thistle foliage background—light green with the new leaves, mottled brown on green in midsummer and finally, in autumn's gravid females, brown to match the plant at the end of its life cycle. The mantis's costuming is too accurate to avoid the speculation that this mutually beneficial relationship with the thistle is an accident.

There is someone else who, I suspect, enjoys a time-blessed liaison with the thistle—the goldfinch. There is probably no more spectacular way to see the thistle than the way Audubon saw it, with a goldfinch riding a ripened seed pod, filling the breeze with a flurry of thistledown. The earliest ripening pods draw the attention of feeding families of goldfinches in July and August. To me, the goldfinch says something about the company the thistle keeps.

In many birds, the food cries of the young seem little more than a demanding *cheep* of gluttony—hardly more appealing (to the human observer) than a brattish banging on the table by an overstuffed child. With the goldfinch, it's different. The food cry is demure and sweet. A violin in the hands of a master is capable of notes almost that clear. The feeding family converse together as a baroque ensemble.

When the thistle's flowers have passed, the seeds mature deep within the urn-shaped pods. Each seed is attached to a wispy airfoil called a pappus which expands when released, the seed and pappus together resembling a streaming comet. Plunging from its roller-coaster flight, the goldfinch attacks the pod just as the downy plumes emerge. The little "wild canary" tears at the down to free the seeds. He gets perhaps one in ten. The autumn wind takes the rest—and plants a few.

2 / *The Stream*

QUITS THE FIELD, we said of the hummingbird, with a chittering swoop. And heads for a habitat which holds tremendous attraction for him and for a great many other creatures. Including you and me when we pause to acknowledge it.

Think back to your last walk through the woods and fields. For how much of your journey did you follow running water?

See if this rings a bell. You walked briskly, at first, feeling your feet kiss the earth. It was good. You took the first few hills apace, blunting the edge of your nervous energy and letting your senses equilibrate with the outdoors. Your perceptions were sky, groups of moving vegetation, the pleasant pull against your leg muscles. Half a mile; perhaps a mile. Then the briars and branches tugged at your clothes and you slowed. You perceived yourself less, your surroundings more. Sounds and smells and dancing life forms queued for attention. Your senses focused—leaves, caterpillars, a circling vulture. You moved deliberately now, alert and receptive. The earth sloped gently away before you through the woods. Soon you heard running water.

The gurgling of the stream in conversation with its rock substrate drew you closer. You moved inexorably toward it, groping, touching, an explorer discovering the rim of some *terra incognita*. You paused for long minutes at the edge of a stream scarcely a yard wide. You studied the tiny pool between the stones, the little spigot of a waterfall six inches high. You began to move slowly upstream—why, you couldn't say—but it was more comfortable than downstream. Your feet followed the water's edge, your eyes followed the waterstriders' jerky errands over the surface film, your face brushed the alder. Ever upstream; ever so slowly. You really couldn't say how long—a quarter of the sun's arc, a doubling of the shadows' length. By and by you were O.K., the stream was O.K. There was the clearing, the hedgerow that leads to the logging road that leads to the big field on the other side of the paved road from home.

Like the raccoon on its nightly patrol and the hummingbird testing a touch-me-not's nectar, humans are subject to the magnetism of a stream. We may not have our fellow foragers' keen awareness of what riches stock a woodland stream, but there we gravitate to seek our beginnings, and to let the stream surprise us as it will.

I'll give you an example. There is a park in Chapel Hill, the town I live in. It is graciously large as small-town parks go— eighty acres, more or less. Its principal claims to beauty are the maturing deciduous woods which tower from its undisturbed slopes and a little stream which cleaves them. The stream runs the length of the park, roughly bisecting it to join with two other rivulets at a spot the villagers once reverently referred to as "the meeting of the waters." Shintoists would have enshrined the little confluence, its beauty being a gift of the spirits. But the good Christians buried it in a series of culverts beneath a football stadium parking lot. And the fern-kissed splashes that once made the hearts of children dance now seep into the storm sewers of progress.

Despite this downstream entombment, a network of pathways penetrates the park's stillness. None is constructed, none even officially sanctioned. The paths have come to define the lines of least resistance—or greatest attraction—to people and other animals traversing the park. You can enter by any of half a dozen trails, but the result is the same: within a hundred yards you are following the stream. All paths lead to the stream and there intersect the main footway. To avoid the stream you must make a conscious effort to counter the flow of the terrain, to resist the stream's field of influence. The route the water takes is not necessarily the most convenient one for walking. At times the way is

15

blocked by the stream's artwork in the rocky outcrops. Still, you struggle happily over the rocks and follow the water's gurgling charisma. The smooth, open wooded slopes above are pathless, untraveled.

As water is the stuff of life in great aggregations like seas and estuaries, it is all the more so in the uplands where smaller volumes of it serve larger spaces. Perhaps it is only human to marvel at a trackless coastal marsh, quartered to the horizon into the fishing territories of white herons, and so neglect the life on the tiny stream behind our home. I cling to this weakness in myself and feel it most keenly when I am by the side of a stream. Any stream.

A stream is a flowing body of water intermediate in size between a brook and a creek. A brook you can jump, a creek you must wade, but a stream you can often cross by stepping on two or three well-placed rocks. In much of North America, a stream is often not more than ten miles long because, in that span, enough brooks flow into it to make it a creek. And it doesn't take many conjoining creeks to make a river.

There is also the consideration of gradient: a stream's slope. Streams can and do occur at all levels of watershed, from the highlands down to the coastal plain. And wherever you find a particular stream on this hyperbolic curve connecting mountains with the sea, gradient dictates the rate of flow; which in turn determines the topography of the stream's bottom and hence the habitat. The waters sprint off the highlands over cleanly polished rocks to meander sluggishly through the coastal plain; dropping more and more of their silt burden as the pace slows. The muddy beds of lazy lowland rivers offer vastly different living conditions than the burnished bottoms of mountain brooks. Since fewer of us live on streams of extreme gradient, either flat or steep, we can most meaningfully consider streams of the midlands. Those with moderate gradients slow enough to permit some bottom vegetation but not slow enough to deposit much silt. The bottom of such a stream would probably have rocks the size of your head, or smaller, alternating with deposits of sand and gravel where the flow slackens.

Flowing water of any sort is but a loop in the Gordian Knot

16

called, for simplicity, the water cycle. The beginning point is usually said to be the ocean, for there a great transformation occurs. Energy from the sun vaporizes water from the ocean's surface, molecule by molecule, purifying and separating it from all dissolved salts and impurities. The water is borne aloft on solar-powered convection currents, to condense with the cooling effect of altitude and eventually to fall again. Most of this water falls back directly into the sea. But winds carry a portion inland to begin a circuitous and sustaining dalliance with the web of upland life. Before this water returns to the sea, it may circulate through underground aquifers, be exhaled back into the air through the leaves of trees, be impounded in lakes, seep into a surface flow, or serve in the cytoplasm of plant and animal cells. Eventually, gravity prevails and the water replenishes the sea, bearing traces of the chemistry and substance of the uplands. We see it in a stream for the merest moment along its endless odyssey.

One more point of description—an intangible. I have wrestled often with the wording of this motion. It is based entirely on feeling. A quickening pulse I get when I hear running water and know that beyond the thicket there must flow a stream. I don't know if streams give anyone else this feeling; I'd feel foolish asking. But I hope I am not alone because the sensation is delicious. It is an uneasy curiosity that possesses me as I pick about in the pools and trickles. Nothing really threatening—but a strangeness that draws me ever closer. Toward I don't know what. I pick up a dripping stone and mayfly naiads scurry in bewilderment as their world turns upside down. Do I see in these living fossils my own larval ancestors? Or am I looking at myself a thousand incarnations hence. Creatures like these were once the planet's most advanced forms, I muse. In whose palm do I squirm when the lights go out and every vestige of human civilization is obliterated in the majesty of a thunderstorm?

But this much is fact. There throbs in every unsullied stream a dense community of living things. It is a tremendous concentration of life in a tiny volume. A still body of water of a stream's dimensions could not possibly be so fecund, else every puddle would seethe and churn. What is the stream's sustaining force? Where do its teeming populations get their energy and nutrients?

17

The answer distinguishes the life systems of an ocean or marsh or pond from those of a stream.

Oceans and marshes and ponds contain their own primary food producers—the plants which trap solar energy and make it palatable to animals and fungi. A stream manufactures only a tiny fraction of its food; its few plants are constantly thinned and uprooted by currents. But no matter. The entire watershed of a stream is its garden. Every drop that trickles off the soil carries with it a ration of decomposing land plants particles. It is the detritus from land plants that gives the stream its food. Dissolved minerals from the watershed provide the nutrients. Water tumbling over rocks becomes richly aerated with dissolved oxygen. Because a stream draws on the resources of its entire watershed, it can sustain a powerful engine of life out of all proportion to its size. This may have something to do with my quickening pulse.

Once the detritus-laden water enters a stream, perhaps by way of a stagnant bottomland pool where it might pick up some plankton, it begins to feed an army of strange creatures. Strange to us because they have no counterparts who walk on land. They seem to be creatures of the deep taken from another age. In terms of the life forms we encounter in our daily perceptions, the beasts of a stream might as well be from another planet.

The surface film alone is a rewarding habitat to explore. Water molecules at the surface of the stream bond tightly together forming a powerful but invisible film. This film will bend to support the weight of a steel needle, giving it a nearly frictionless cushion on which to align with the earth's magnetic field and thus serve as a crude compass. The same molecular forces draw our body fluids through tiny capillaries and hold small volumes of falling water together in drops. Numerous creatures of the stream make their home at this two-dimensional frontier of air and water.

The waterstrider is probably the most familiar. There are many species throughout North America. All are of the order Hemiptera, the true bugs. For most of my life I noticed waterstriders scooting gaily over the quiet backwaters, casting their big-footed shadows on the bottom. I never gave a thought to how they made their living until two summers ago, when I captured several to photograph them. As I leaned over to focus on one strider, hoping to catch the glare which outlines the depressions their feet make in the surface film, it leapt straight into the air and returned to the surface sucking the juices from a gnat. And so I learned that the striders' seemingly playful skatings over the surface are really the hunting sweeps of a predator. The literature describes waterstriders as being devourers of aquatic insects snagged just below the surface, as well as terrestrial insects which fall to the water. They even feast upon their own nymphs.

Some species of waterstriders are winged and take to the air to seek better conditions when drought or hunger threaten. A six-inch leap into the air after prey is common, but observers doubt the wings come into play for that purpose. The main source of locomotion is the powerful sweeping of the middle pair of legs. Tufts of hair at the tips of these legs serve as paddles while the rear legs steer the careening insect. The front limbs are mantis-like vices for grasping prey.

Waterstriders prey on insects trapped by the surface film or swimming beneath it.

Whirligigs! The instant you seem them you know there can't be any other name for them. They are little beetles resembling watermelon seeds that zoom in erratic circles over the surface film. Somehow the individuals in this gyrating mass avoid collision, perhaps through the same harmonics that permit galaxies to pass through one another in perfect mesh. The whirligigs are truly versatile. If they are frightened while foraging for food on the surface, they dive. As with all beetles, the forewings are modified into hardened plates, called elytra, which cover the frilly hindwings at rest. Whirligigs store air under their elytra for prolonged dives. Amazingly, whirligigs are also strong fliers. The

19

only trick of locomotion they appear not to have mastered is that of taking off from the water's surface. But the same molecular tension that keeps them afloat also binds them to the stream. They must climb onto land or vegetation to launch an airborne escape.

To help whirligigs get the best advantages available on both sides of the surface film, their eyes are divided, half of each compound eye providing visual coverage above, half surveying the submerged world. Watching them from below in an aquarium gives a fascinating perspective. One pair of oarlike legs propels them, flashing out at intervals to send the owner in a new direction at each thrust. Whirligigs are thought to be the garbagemen of the stream's surface, lunching on the dead and decaying animal matter imprisoned by the film's force. Studies have revealed that they also obtain live meals both on and below the surface.

I have tried several times to film vignettes of the drama of a stream's food web. In a quiet backwater pool fed by a rain-swollen stream, a water spider grabbed and fanged a careless waterstrider before my camera. The spider had rested motionless for half an hour, with its hind legs anchored to the bank vegetation and some of its forward limbs on the surface film. Water-spiders are recognized by their dorsal rows of white spots against a dark field and by their aquatic habits. When frightened they, too, duck under the surface film to take refuge amidst bottom vegetation, carrying with them on their abdomens a silvery coating of air. Air carried with the diver in this fashion has a "fishes and loaves" quality about its oxygen content. The oxygen in the bubble attracts other molecules of oxygen dissolved in the water, thus replenishing itself. Because the spider, like insects, breathes through pores along its abdomen, the oxygen is readily accessible and adequate for his safety.

I had read about aquatic snails traversing the surface film, but somehow I didn't expect to witness the aquabatics which, for a lumbering gastropod, must pass for daredeviltry. But in the same pool with the water spider, a snail came chugging along, supported on the underface of the surface film. The displacement of the snail's body no doubt buoyed it considerably; I have to doubt that the same feat is possible on the upper surface. Having collected all the condiments it desired from the glassy limit of its watery world, the snail abruptly released itself from the film and tumbled to the algae-coated vegetation below. So I know the animal was not totally supported by its own buoyancy. Like many creatures I will probably never know about, and few I will, the snail had learned to use this seemingly fragile membrane between two worlds.

Gulliver, a normal-sized human, encountered races of people larger and smaller than himself by some orders of magnitude. Through these contrasts he discovered, among other things, the fallacy of presuming his own size scale to be central. Alice, the traveler of Lewis Carroll's fantasies, adjusted her size to that of her hosts. And in so doing, she met many interesting characters on their own terms—her attitude and stature deepening the communication. Both distortions gave the adventurers new perspectives on their real worlds, on themselves.

We could meet the creatures who live beneath the surface of a stream by uprooting their carefully constructed (or selected) little dwellings and dragging them dripping and bewildered from their world into ours. Unfortunately, in practice there really is no alternative, except perhaps to simulate a stream community in an aquarium at home. But who would deny us a brief, fanciful lapse if by that simple expedient we could meet the stream denizens in their own world. Our fantasy; their realism.

And so we sink with the snail to the bottom of our backwater pool. We are little people, an inch high. The snail goes its way, grazing algae from the rocks and plants. We go ours, exploring.

It happens to be spring. We make our way around the edge of the pool seeking the stream's main flow, but big clear masses of jellied beach balls block our way. Frog eggs. We climb over some, around others. At each step we sink to our knees in a cloud of silt. A huge black balloon bears down on us through the murk, a thrashing tail driving it past us at breakneck speed. The bloated form rumbles past, its bow-waves shoving us aside. Some of the frog eggs have hatched.

We grope onward, nearly weightless in the silt. A disc of light beckons. We approach through swirling chunks of vegetable debris. Finally, the coppery headlight is nearly close enough to

21

touch. It is an eye. Squinting through the confetti, we follow the outline of a head—as tall as we are, with its chin in the muck. It's a snake! The skin is a jigsaw puzzle of plates as big as this page. Too close for anything but hope, we look for holes in the monstrous head. A nostril. The eye. But no sensory pit between them. Whew! It's just a water snake; not poisonous. Here the fantasy weakens; poisonous or not, the snake would be unlikely to pass up a one-inch morsel of tasty protein. To survive this situation we had best suppose that, even shrunken to an inch, the human presence strikes fear (or revulsion) into the animal heart. Like a derailed freight train, the snake thrashes to escape. We are knocked into a dream of tumbling creatures and debris, wheeling weightless in the turbulence. A leech cartwheels around us, elongating, shortening, wildly groping with suckers at both ends for a purchase on something fixed. It is only a muscle with a stomach inside, but this simple arrangement can fill itself with five times its mass in vertebrate blood, more than we Lilliputians can afford to donate.

A salamander wiggles past. It was rousted by the flailing snake (who would love to have found the little amphibian) from its resting spot in the silt where it feeds on bits of organic matter. As it swirls above us, we see the blood gills between the head and forelegs and know it is a young salamander, an eft. The light from above makes the red frills glow for an instant, telling us something about the purity of the water. The gills are rather small, indicating a rich oxygen content. Efts living in oxygen-poor waters develop enlarged gills to increase the area over which blood and water-borne oxygen can make contact. At maturity the eft will become a mud salamander three times our length. It will breathe air through internal lungs, but will never venture more than a few feet from the stream, returning there to escape danger, to reproduce, and to feed on insect larvae.

The water snake's siltstorm subsides. We resume our trek toward flowing water, aware from the eft's oxygen indicators that we are exploring a healthy stream. A thriving lotic community awaits us.

We gave some thought earlier to the "strangeness" of some stream creatures, which adds to a stream's mystique—a strange-

Her protecting stream-side rock lifted for the photograph, a salamander guards her nearly-hatched eggs. The yellow areas visible through the egg membranes are the undersides of the young.

ness mostly the result of our unfamiliarity with them. There is a group of ancient but unrelated insects whose stream-dwelling larvae are strange in a less subjective dimension. These are the stoneflies, the mayflies and the caddisflies. Artists' reconstructions

23

of life in the carboniferous period often show these insects perched on horsetails and huge clubmosses. That was two hundred million years ago, when coal was being formed. They had then recently evolved into flying insects with land-based larvae. Sometime later the larvae become aquatic. However, the adults remain basically unchanged to this day. Here's the strange part. We have all heard the early biological tongue-twister: "ontogeny repeats phylogeny." I still have to look up both words every time I see them. Ontogeny: the biological development of an individual. Phylogeny: the evolutionary development of a species. Decoded, the expression means that the development of an individual re-enacts the evolution of its kind. Gill slits and rudimentary tails on fetal humans are examples; humankind once evolved through these stages. Well, mayflies, stoneflies and caddisflies violate this principle. These insect orders developed with terrestrial larvae; but today's individuals mature from aquatic naiads that show no evidence of their terrestrial heritage.

There are similarities in the behavior and appearance of these three types of naiads, if not in their taxonomy. They occupy all ranges of current velocity and bottom habitat, eating largely what the current brings, though some are predaceous. Usually they are found under stones. A stone the size of a grapefruit taken from moderate rapids could easily yield several of each.

But when you're an inch high, you don't pick up stones that size. You peer under them. We edge into the stream's flow. Carefully. The footing is precarious. It is like trying to walk in a windstorm holding an umbrella. Using every hand and foothold, we inch toward center stream where the current races even faster. Finally, our strength is inadequate. We find that the only way we can keep from being swept away is to let the water press us against a rock. We soon notice that we are not alone nor is our method of clinging unique: a stone-fly nymph, two-thirds our size, emerges from beneath the stone to inspect us. Its body is a flattened hydrodynamic arch. Working like the slats in venetian blinds, its legs deflect water upward. The faster the current, the more securely the nymph is bound to the rock. It moves casually, but keeps its head upstream. It fondles us with two long antennae which appear to be balanced at its other end by two whiplike tail

24

filaments. Trachial gills filled with air tubes (instead of blood vessels like the eft's gills) befrill its underparts. On the sides of the streamlined head, two large compound eyes flank three dots, the ocelli, arranged in a centered triangle. The body is attractively colored with darkly trimmed yellow.

Two hundred fifty adult species of stoneflies are known in the United States, but only half their nymphs have been identified. Reflecting the attrition of the ages, there are numerous genera with only one surviving species, several families with but a few members.

The life cycles most familiar to us feature relatively short stages of immaturity and growth followed by long and productive adulthoods. With stoneflies this is not the case. Nor with mayflies or caddisflies. Stonefly nymphs haunt the stream bottoms for from one to three years before emerging as flying adults. The adult stage lasts only a fortnight or so, during which mating and egg-laying are considerably more important than eating. The adults tend to appear at very specific times—usually the colder months—and are rarely found far from running water. They are often seen clinging to vegetation at the edge of a stream, into which they deposit their eggs after mating. Some species actually re-enter the water as adults to attach their eggs to stones on the bottom.

The stonefly's major involvement with the stream community takes place during its prolonged larval adolescence. The individual whose boulder we share has turned its attention from us to a smaller nymph. It is generally similar to the stonefly but its tail is adorned with *three* whiplike filaments, identifying it as a mayfly nymph. A row of trachial gills flaps rhythmically along each side of its abdomen. Its hydrodynamic body contour is so effective that its belly forms a suction cup against the stone. The two larvae smell and feel one another with their antennae. The stonefly's sensors tell it "food" just as the mayfly's telegraph "danger." The stonefly seizes its prey and retires beneath the rock to feast.

The mayfly's presence confirms the eft's oxygen analysis. Some species of stoneflies live in lakes and pools, but mayflies live only in well-aerated running water, the cleaner the better.

25

Twin tail filaments identify the naiad of the stonefly. Trachial gills befrill the thorax between the hydro-dynamically-shaped legs.

The mayfly's life cycle adds another notch of strangeness. It is the only insect to molt after it flies. Every other flying insect is considered "mature" at first flight. Having endured the countless perils of a larval youth and the final alchemy of metamorphosis,

the insects are finished with growth and change when their wings unfold. The mayfly is different. After perhaps twenty larval molts over three years, the mature larva rises to the stream's surface. The skin splits and there emerges a stage uniquely the mayfly's —the subimago. It is a pale version of the real adult. A few hours and aerial gyrations later, the subimago molts again and the mature mayfly joins the mating horde in nuptial flight.

Adulthood for the mayfly—the only phase people see unless they are an inch high or unless they fritter away their time picking up rocks from streambeds—is ephemeral. It lasts only a few hours, or perhaps a day or two, depending on the species. The order to which they belong is called Ephemeroptera. Reproduction is the sole function of the adult. It doesn't eat. It doesn't even have any mouth parts. It mates, lays eggs and dies. Some even return to the current-swept bottom of a stream to oviposit on the underside of a rock. Once I waded into a promising stream on a spring day, picked up a stone and found a mature female mayfly clinging to it. On almost every other stone I pulled from the racing current, the wet sail of a mayfly's wings caught the sun. But I saw no other mayflies in the air, none resting on streamside plants. Only females depositing eggs in neat geometric patterns on the underside of stones the size of grapefruits. Very strange.

We move on. Or attempt to. Our feet get caught in a sticky web resembling a basketball net. A wormy thing with bladelike jaws emerges from a niche to inspect its catch. It is a caddisfly nymph. This creature feeds on the organisms its net strains from the flow. We hastily shake free. The caddis larva finds its net torn but empty. It repairs the web, secreting from its mouth a sticky thread which hardens on contact with water. Several tiny freshwater clam larvae, fist-sized pearls, shimmer in the net, safe in their shells. Legs, shells, antennae, other bits and pieces of bygone meals bedeck the case in which the caddis nymph awaits a tug at its net.

We rest in the lee of a large stone. The currents have sorted out and deposited there a uniform collection of pebbles—all only waist-high to us. Then one of the pebbles begins to move. We see that it is not really a single pebble but a collection of tiny chips of stone cemented together to form a protective case. A

Laced to a stream-bottom rock, the catch net of a caddisfly larva sifts animal prey from the current. The caddis larva (at the lower center of the net) inspects what appears to be a captured larval clam.

blackish head and legs protrude from the open end, gathering in algae and other organic material. This is another species of caddisfly larva. In our fanciful trek along the stream bottom we might find many species—there are seven hundred fifty known in the United States—but only a small portion are recognized as larvae, even by experts. The case design is unique to each (case-building) species. Those living in rapid currents use heavier materials; those favoring still waters enshroud themselves in bits of plant matter.

Bending to examine this wormlike larva, we peer into its case. A thick exoskeleton shields the head and thorax. The abdomen, always protected by the case, is soft. Frilly trachial gills protrude from the abdominal segments, waving water through the case. Three spacing knobs on the thorax keep the body centered in its case so that water can flow through. Glands near the front of the body produce glue to cement new bits of rock to the open end of the case as the larva grows. An immense trout—really only eight inches long—notices the movement and gobbles up the nymph, case and all. Its digestive tract will separate stone from flesh.

A great boulder looms ahead. It is covered by a bright green mantle of freshwater sponge. Like its marine counterpart, the freshwater sponge is a very primitive animal, filtering its food from the water through countless openings. A caddis larva, apparently a sponge specialist, has channeled causeways through the porous animal. It needs no case, for its body does not protrude above the level of the sponge. Most caddis larvae are dark and colorless; this sponge-eater is a polished turquoise.

Ahead we see the blunt-nosed outline of a fish three times our length resting motionless on the bottom, head upstream, its pectoral fins gripping the gravel. It is called a darter. A tiny mayfly nymph runs up the side of a stone. The fish darts toward the nymph. We watch the nymph in the split second before the fish strikes and see what may be the only known use of the tail filaments. It whips them together for a burst of speed not quite adequate to escape the darter. The fish devours the nymph and sinks back immediately onto the gravel. Behind a mask of immobility, its form vanishes into the background.

Asian farmers often wear a hat of straw woven into a gentle cone. Clinging to a rock in the turbulent waters, we see just such a hat. It would fit us perfectly if it were not already occupied. It is the water penny, aquatic child of an inconspicuous land beetle. It is the size of a big person's fingernail and just as hard. The margins of the coppery shell form a suction cup that seals the larva against the contour of the stone, immune to the ripping current and probably to most predation. The water penny glides slowly over the rock gleaning organic matter from its surface. At our touch it flattens like a manhole cover welded to the stone.

This current-swept bottom, which we might slosh through as big people and assume to be lifeless, is really a veritable zoo of alien creatures. We proceed cautiously, for many are voracious predators. There is the hellgrammite, larva of the dobsonfly. It looks like a creation from a creepy critters kit. Rows of spikes bristle from its wormlike body. Its fearsome head is armed with jaws that can painfully nip a full-sized human. In our present configuration it could easily shear through an arm or a leg. And there is the larva of the delicate damselfly, recognized by the three trachial gills protruding from its tail like a cluster of willow leaves. The nymph preys on other aquatic larvae; the iridescent adults hawk flying insects above the stream.

Finally, we meet the most voracious predator among, and on, the aquatic larvae; the dragonfly naiad. Knobby eyes bulge from the sides of its toadlike head. Its dark, wide form battles the current with jets of water from an aft-aimed breathing port. This panther of the rapids moves past us and disappears beneath the boulder. Suddenly the sides of the rock are acrawl with fleeing stonefly and mayfly nymphs. A darter arrives as if shot from a cannon and picks off several of the fugitives. A stonefly waves its antennae in confusion, weighing, we imagine, the risk of exposure to passing fish against the monster which has usurped the stone's protective underside. Suddenly the stonefly is seized from below by a mechanical device resembling those geometric fire tongs that reach out as they close—the lower lip of the dragonfly nymph. Hinged in several places, it folds beneath the head while not in use, but lunges half the nymph's length to fasten and retrieve prey.

We have passed center stream. Now the bottom slopes upward; the current slackens. The raging waters of some previous storm anchored a log against the bank. A sandy shoal spreads in its lee. In several spots, bits of detritus—swirling like time-lapse footage of solar flares—mark a flow into and out of the sand. We approach and examine. Two huge shells are separated by a long, fringe-lined slit into which water is flowing. A steady flow pours out of an adjacent oval opening, bearing considerably less detritus than the water on its way in. These are the intake and outlet siphons of a freshwater clam. We dig around the shell but find no head, no eyes, no antennae. We do find a "foot," a muscular blob which wedges its way into the sand, expands laterally, then contracts in length to hunch the clam forward.

Even if we had seen no fish along our fanciful trek, the clam confirms their presence in the stream. Fish are essential to the propagation of freshwater mussels. To reproduce, the male mussels release sperm into the water which fertilizes eggs in females downstream. The eggs hatch in a pouch under the protection of the females' shells and the tiny larval mussels are expelled into the current. The stream's entire population of mussels would eventually wind up in the ocean if these seemingly dull creatures hadn't evolved one the cleverest adaptations to streambed living. The larvae are born with the impulse to snap the halves of their shells shut at the slightest disturbance. A passing minnow foraging on the bottom is apt to brush an infant mussel with a fin which the bivalve clamps onto, eventually burrowing into the fish's tissue as a parasite. The trip upstream then becomes a *snap*,

30

as it were. After a few weeks in the host fish (which can easily carry a number of encysted clam larvae with no ill effects), the mussel emerges and falls to the bottom. Happiness for a larval clam is ejecting over a sandbar in clear water rich in detritus and protozoans.

We pause for a while, musing on the life and times of our monster clam. The sand heaves and the clam plows powerfully forward half its length. We see the concentric ridges in its shell, laid down during alternate periods of stress and growth. We wonder how old it is, where it boarded its private submarine, where it got off, and where it has traveled since.

The reverie is nearly our undoing. A crawfish has discovered us. Long buggywhip antennae caress and smell us. We look up in horror at a nightmare of claws, pincers and flailing mechanical parts towering over us. We never saw quite so clearly why the crawfish is classified a decapod: ten legs probe and grasp and grab at everything around and under it, passing chunks of who knows what from claw to claw to feeding palp even though the monster is fully intent at the moment on devouring us. The great lobster lunges forward!

We have encountered the most voracious predator-scavenger of the stream bottom. The crawfish will eat anything, anytime, dead or alive. In our diminutive form, we can survive this situation only by some absurd old-time cowboy movie escape which would trouble our credulity more than it would help us experience an alien habitat. The fantasy has served us well enough until now, but finally placed us in an aquatic cul-de-sac. We must retreat into reality. To escape the monster lobster, we outgrow it.

We are people-size once again. It was intrepid of you to accompany me along the stream bottom, especially since I really had no idea how it would work out. If I still hold your trust, let me offer another device for getting to know a stream's creatures, one considerably less dangerous. We will simulate a stream community in an aquarium.

A moment ago the crawfish was rubbing its feeding palps together in hungry anticipation. Now it fondles our rubber boot tips apprehensively. Pick it up, if you will. Carefully, with a thumb and forefinger on each side of the carapace behind the head. Even

31

with our adjustment in size, those pincers can still draw blood. Dripping and flipping its tail in the air, the little decapod gropes in frustration for something to pinch hell out of. Into the bucket he goes, darting backward and threatening with raised claws.

With a light seine you can collect a few of the fish racing about the stream. Anyone will tell you they are "minnows." That's a broad colloquial category which includes daces, shiners, and chubs. A half-dozen fish in your tank will be enough. If you find more than one species, a pair of each will suffice. If you have any luck working your net, you will get a variety of individuals to choose from, so be on the lookout for little black dots in the fins and tails. That's a fish with mussel parasites.

The only reliable way to find live clams is the raccoon method —you have to feel around the sand and gravel bars with your forepaws. When you have the technique down pat, you can look distractedly off into the distance while briskly working the bottom with your fingers. Just like a raccoon.

You'll want a few surface critters—whirligigs, waterstriders. Take a snail or two. And make a liberal collection of may-, stone- and caddisfly larvae. One each of the predators like dragon-, damsel- and dobsonfly larvae will do. Efts like to hide under fist-sized stones resting in coarse sand. They do well in an aquarium. *If* separated by a glass pane or screen from the crawfish. (This goes for darters, too.) You will want one or two hefty stones, so find one with a water penny on it.

Some stream denizens simply cannot adapt to an aquarium so it is unfair to collect them. Sponges die very quickly as do hydra and blackfly larvae. They need a rapid flow, and apparently nothing short of a lotic habitat will sustain them. In general, anything you take from the rapids will probably die in an aquarium for lack of food and oxygen. It is best to collect in calmer waters.

The bottom material is important. It provides hiding places and usually some silt and detritus for the guests in your tank. I suggest grading the size of your substrate across the tank's length, from coarse sand to heavy gravel. The animals will select the type bottom they like. Expect some bonus critters in your bottom material. A shovel of gravel could well contain a number of leeches, efts, worms and aquatic beetle grubs. Plus a few creatures you will never be able to identify.

A ten-gallon tank, a light, pump, filter and airstone is all the equipment you need. Fifteen dollars should outfit you handsomely unless we move into three-digit inflation before this book gets to press. Forget the plants. You don't need them unless the community you are trying to duplicate—and you will only be able to make a crude approximation anyway—features plants.

One thing is a must. Fill the tank with stream water. It may surprise you, but your tap water is far too filthy. To counteract the filth, it probably contains additives which will quickly float your collection to the surface, belly up.

Now you are in the observation business. *Some* of the behavior of *some* of your creatures will be just about what it would be in the stream. People who have aquariums full of store-bought fish tend to perceive the setup much as they would background music: they're aware there is something alive in the tank and that's about all. They drop in some store-bought food every now and then and watch the sluggish Pavlovian response. I warrant you won't be able to take this approach with your stream setup. You'll spend hours watching, involved, fascinated. There will be creatures molting, fighting, mating, hatching, hunting, killing and eating. Some will die, some will thrive, some will dominate. You will soon begin to see some of the relationships and interrelationships. Contrived and unbalanced as it is, you will see that what you have on your hands is a life system. They don't sell those in pet shops.

With the size ratio improved and some glass between us, we are ready to deal with the crawfish. Ten legs it has. But that's not the half of it. In all, the crawfish senses and manipulates its surroundings with nineteen pairs of appendages. The body suggests a contrivance out of the machine age. Beginning at the head are two vertically matched small antennae (antennules). Then come the long antennae. Then five pairs of appendages for handling and shredding food. The big fighting and prey-grabbing claws (chelae) are next, followed by four sets of walking legs. The first two pairs are clawed, the last two end in hooks. Further aft are five pairs of swimmerets which fan water under the tail segments. Finally come two pairs of uropods and a telson, the five elements of the tail fan used for quick rearward escape.

The feeding mechanism is a marvel of adaptability. It lets the crawfish dine on a range of fare. The "crawdad" can hold a minnow to its mandibles and gnaw out great chunks or it can mince decomposing matter with its palps and fan the shreds into its gullet with the "bailers," the second maxillae. You often see these organs flailing under the crawfish's chin to keep a flow of water moving over the internal gills.

Assigning a sex to a creature is a weakness which afflicts me. But for creatures of character, "it" just seems inadequate. The demeanor usually suggests a gender somehow. Crawfish are easily sexed, however, if you can compare them. Males have the larger claws, the narrower bodies. Females are markedly broad.

Your crawfish may be missing a leg or may lose one after entering your tank (in which case it will probably eat the limb; when the time comes to shed its skin and grow, it will eat that, too). A lost limb is no cause for alarm. The second joint of each leg is calibrated to break off easily and is just as easily regenerated. Fights often result in lost limbs. I once found a huge pincer broken off in a stream. It must have been an inch long. I was wading barefoot at the time, so I tried not to think about the pincers on the victor in that encounter.

I stand on bone-dry rocks in the streambed and listen to the endless drone of summer. The yodeling clucks of a raincrow counterpoint the cicadas' rasp. The water is low. My feet straddle a stone the size of a grapefruit. Its top bakes; its bottom stews in a quiet pool an inch deep. I vaguely feel that I was once pressed against that stone with a stonefly naiad and a friend. The stream now seeps and trickles. Its creatures aestivate. I wish I could.

A few white clots of cumulus look up at me from the blue pool. I study the sky's reflection in the center, the circus of trees around the pool's edge. A huge oak fell across the stream in a spring storm some years ago. Its falling opened a gap in the canopy above the stream so that I can see the sky in the pool at my feet. And so that the colony of touch-me-nots can huddle in the sun-

Amid a flurry of detritus, the stream's energy source, a crawfish devours a dace. The dark dots on the fish's skin and scales are the encysted larvae of fresh-water clams who, harm-lessly, use the fish for upstream transportation.

light on the gravel bar before me like players on a lighted stage, a debauchery of orange bangles on their branch tips. The flowers are shaped like tiny trumpets with curly tails.

Past my head sails the mad swooper, chittering. I look up

35

The cardinal flower, growing along stream banks in eastern North America, depends on hummingbird pollination. (As the bill thrusts into the fused corolla after nectar, the flower's sexual parts, located on the white-tipped structures above the petals, tap the bird's forehead to make the pollen exchange.)

and see the ruby-radiant throat pulsing sweetness from the nectaries deep in the orange trumpets. The needlelike bill thrusts deep; the forehead touches the stygmas. Pollen from another touch-me-not settles in to germinate. Some of this flower's pollen powders the bird's forehead. Every time this happens I marvel at my good luck that the hummingbird just happened to zoom in on these flowers at this moment. Luckier still that it should visit the very closest blossoms to me. Then I remember it isn't a question of lucky timing. It's the ruby-throat's way of protesting a disturbance in his territory.

Another swoop; another flower. This one is red. Incredibly red. The cardinal flower. The bill jabs vertically down the blood-hued corolla; white sexual parts reach up and tap the bird's forehead, exchanging pollen. In the wash of whirring wings, the leaves dance for a moment against the dog-day's stillness. The tiny bird genuflects into flower after flower, plant after plant.

The cardinal flower and the touch-me-not grow only along streams. They are pollinated mostly by hummingbirds. The stream-hummingbird association is strengthened further by the bird's frequent selection of nest sites in low branches overhanging streams. It is through the hummingbird, the hiking human, and half a hundred other birds and animals that a stream relates to the land it drains.

Nothing gladdens the trout fisherman's mendacious heart like the raucous rattle of a kingfisher speeding upstream under the arched alders. The rod stops midcast, the leader fouls, the eyes follow the bullet-fast blue, the ears hear the dopplershifted remonstrance clatter past. The kingfisher is a voluble, visible adjunct to a winding watercourse. If streams could all get together and elect a mascot, it would be the kingfisher. Stroking the air with fitful irregularity, jabbering petulantly, the kingfisher dives headlong into the rushing waters and then flies to an alder perch to down its minnow. With a stream creature's characteristic iconoclasm, the kingfisher perforates a maxim. Male birds are more brightly colored than female birds, right? Right. Except for kingfishers. The bird nests in a cavity excavated in a streambank. The incubating female has no need of drab protective coloration, nor the male need of gaudy colors to distract predators from the nest. Consequently, the female wears a rusty cumberbund across her girth which the male lacks. We might fancy that, with the need for protective plumage minimized, natural selection has permitted the kingfishers whatever colors please them. A happy thought—kingfishers look exactly as they would like.

Often in summer the green heron will flush from its fishing rock at the stream's edge and CHAK a loud protest at your intrusion. This little fisherman differs from other egrets and herons in that it is more of a climber than a wader and is thus better adapted to hunting from rocks and fallen logs in the flowing water than are its relatives. Green herons visit our streams regularly in the warm months, skulking stealthily along the banks and shoals, neck hunched in and ready at any moment to plunge the rapier bill forward to skewer fish or frog. The extended neck effectively doubles the bird's length and completely changes its appearance. The feet are well adapted for grasping, so that the little heron can hang almost vertically from a fishing perch, lunge headfirst into the water, and then return with its catch to the upright, hunched posture without once changing its grip on the perch.

My favorite field guide to birds lists the Louisiana waterthrush as "uncommon," which means that, unless you look knowledgeably for the bird, you may go a lifetime without seeing it. Unless, of course, you refresh your spirits by the streamside where, throughout the Northeast, you can find them nesting at frequent intervals. The waterthrush, actually a warbler rather than a true thrush, grooms the gravel bars and rapids, poking its head into

37

the water for worms and insect larvae, all the while dancing a charming little hula. The bird is constantly in motion and prone to cover great stretches of stream in a feeding foray.

Naturally, the intensity of life below a stream's surface attracts lively predator populations along its banks. Reptiles and amphibians figure prominently in the food network which helps redistribute some of a stream's wealth back to the adjacent land. Terrapins lumber through the wooded bottomlands and pass the sultry days snoozing in the cool mud. Snapping turtles wait in watery ambush. Frogs camp on mossy banks to gulp insects and leap into the current when danger threatens. When their sense of timing fails, they end up in the gullets of a variety of bird and animal predators. Snakes eat a variety of aquatic vertebrates, including lizards, salamanders, frogs and one another. The snakes in turn feed higher predators. Hawks and owls take snakes. Apparently some mammals do, too. I once found a mostly eaten watersnake on a streambed rock. The flesh had been stripped neatly from between the ribs. Hawks and owls swallow their prey whole and later regurgitate the undigestables—hair, scales, feathers, bone—in a wad. These pellets record the raptor's diet. You can easily pick them apart and tell hair from feathers, bird bone from mammal bone (bird bones tend to be long, thin, hollow). For the past three years, I have watched a pair of barred owls nest in the park I described earlier. Often their pellets contain crawfish claws and carapace. Big ones. I'd sure hate to swallow them whole. Nesting in an ancient sycamore by the stream, the owls have developed a taste for crawdads.

A stream's mammals are shy and usually nocturnal. They jealously guard the secret of their daytime whereabouts but are generous with information on who was where last night. Their tracks, their leavings (a rock overturned, a crawfish den dug out) and their droppings tell all that you would know if you had watched the nightly traffic through the eyes of an owl. The droppings are especially expressive. They are almost always used as territorial markers. It makes sense; running water would quickly neutralize the scent left by tracks or urine, so a visual marker is necessary. A prominent stone in the water or a fallen log bridg-

38

ing the flow is likely to bear these markings and to have them renewed after each period of high water. The authors are very effectively telling their neighbors, "This is my favorite fishing spot and I better not find you on it next time I come back."

Once a spot becomes so marked, it may collect numerous calling cards. This begins to suggest the sharing of a fishing log by several raccoons, let's say, who may not require sole rights but want other users to know they have a stake in the matter. These communications may cross ethnic lines. I have found scats from three species—mink, raccoon, and a caller whose credentials I did not recognize—on a logjam. The same *square foot* of the log. Since there appeared to be only one dropping from each, I think the possibility should be considered that this was an interspecific communique. Now, I humbly submit, that is profound.

I don't mean to prolong the clinical aspects of this type of observation, but a wholesome grasp of scatology is among a naturalists's most valuable tools. There is at least one good field guide available on animal tracks and scats, and I consider it indispensable. The size and shape of the scats identify the author, the contents recount his diet. Once the scats have weathered and dried a bit, they are not messy and can be pulled apart without a wrinkle of the most fastidious nose. There's nothing strange about inspecting animal droppings. That's what they are left for.

The raccoon is regarded as the godfather of a stream community. It is the dominant predator, keen of wit and sense, elusive and—ask any 'coon dog—a mean fighter. A relative of the peaceful panda, the raccoon exerts primacy over all other stream creatures, prey and predator alike. Anyone who can gnaw open a clam, catch a frog in midleap, and escape in a flash to any number of streamside den trees—regardless of the present occupant's wishes—needs little else by way of introduction.

The raccoon's comings and goings—published daily in the tracks on the sandbars, the empty clam shells, the fecal markings —meter a stream's health. Being top predator, it fares well only if a strong life system nurtures its prey. Sandbars embroidered with 'coon tracks cry out, "Come play in these waters. Splash and refresh. There is life here." That you could swear the tracks were made by a human infant on all fours makes the invitation all the more convincing.

Streams without 'coon tracks are sick. Report their absence at once to your county commissioners, your aldermen. Raccoons abound on practically every stream, even within municipal limits, except where humanity's much lower sanitary standards exclude them. Theirs is a gourmet world of shellfish and fingerbowls, escargot, frog's legs and petite lobsters. Filthy up their streams and they decamp.

Someone speculated that life on earth will finally flicker out on the eternal snows of Ecuador with the last insect preening its antennae under a weak red sun. Insects were among the earliest animals; the prophet says they shall be the last. The existence of mammals spans fewer eons. They arrived later and will disappear sooner than the durable insects. Individual mammal species (including *Homo-you-know-who*) don't last long at all. But there is one mammal whose contempt for time is legend. The opossum.

This ancient omnivore foraged along paleocene streams sixty million years ago when it was in the vanguard of mammal development. Whole orders of mammalian life have come and gone while the North American opossum plodded ungracefully and relentlessly through the quiet backwaters, dimly sensing the flow of riches past its nose. Contrast with the raccoon is total. The raccoon is the stream's epicure, the opossum its garbage man. It will eat absolutely anything. The raccoon is all razzle-dazzle, the opossum dense and pedestrian. Corner a raccoon and you go to the hospital. Approach a 'possum and it goes into a defenseless catatonia. But don't make the mistake of putting one in the cage with your pet rabbit. By the next morning, every single shred of rabbit will have passed through the opossum whom you will find curled in a corner regarding the world with a dull stare.

How this anachronism has survived is not for us to know. Something may ask the same about us someday. But for more eons than you and I have fingers and toes, the opossum—binding water to land, epoch to epoch—has prowled this continent's streams. Let us venture a crude prediction. As long as North

America's waters are warm enough to flow to the sea, the opossum will waddle the streambanks, drooling bits of snail shell. It was probably the first mammal to do so. It may be the last.

A principal predator and the undisputed epicure of a stream's food web, a raccoon dines on frog legs.

3 / *Spring Ephemerals*

THERE IS A GROUP of ten or twelve species of wildflowers called the spring ephemerals. They live on the forest floor below the towering deciduous canopies of temperate North America. They are very beautiful; but more than beautiful, they are very special in the time and place of their being. They have zeroed in on a lifestyle which is downright enterprising, and they live by a precise schedule that would impress the commuter who must make an 8:10 train each morning. Theirs is a fascinating story, but it cannot be told without a digression to set the mind thinking in terms of biologic time.

The earliest stirrings of human intellect may have focused on the movements of heavenly bodies. Certainly the thrust of primitive science was toward celestial events and a mathematics by which to explain them. Archaeologists are forever unearthing new finds to show that ancient societies achieved precise methods of predicting these celestial events. To know that the builders of Stonehenge could predict lunar and solar eclipses to within a few minutes stupefies me, as it must have the average man on the moors thirty-eight hundred years ago. If this degree of sophistication was achieved that long ago, it must have been in the morning twilight of the human experience that the first shaman observed towards the end of the season of bitterest cold, there comes a day of equal parts light and darkness. And that thereafter the days lengthen to a maximum, then shorten to another equinox just before the cold weather resumes. Cro-Magnon, perhaps even Neanderthal man, first related these rudimentary celestial events to seasonal change.

But the deed was done. A calendar was constructed and the sweeps of the sun and moon dominated its face. Societies began to think in terms of seasons defined by celestial movements.

This approach has both strengths and defects. I think it leaves something unsaid to declare that today is the first day of summer because yesterday the sun tracked across the sky at its northern limit. Or that I know winter has begun because last night was the longest night of the year. The recitation of celestial rhythms mentions only the cause. It is the *effect* that living organisms on earth must deal with. And how we *deal* with the effect, the changing sunlight ration (and resulting weather), speaks directly of how we make our living as a species. Of the node we occupy in the circulation of solar energy. Of our ecological niche.

Every day in the lives of Farley Mowat's Ihalmiut is spent in preparation for or in exaltation of four yearly movements of the barren-lands caribou. The people's lives are tied inextricably to the migrations of the deer. June and January mean nothing to them. It might be better if they meant a trifle less to us; if the seasonal prattle of the mockingbird—as vociferous in Central Park as in north Georgia—meant a little more.

But the Gregorian calendar dominates our time sense. We divide our year arbitrarily into months, paint crescents on the calendar to show the moon's phases, and underscore the device's imprecision with an extra day every fourth year. We schedule our celebrations for the fourth Thursday in November or the first Sunday after the first full moon after the vernal equinox. (Easter, believe it or not). But we wouldn't think to call home to wish the old folks well on the day the migrating geese fly over.

There is an alternative. We can divide the year, not into seasons based on celestial cycles, but into aspects which celebrate events in earthy biology. Well-known events. Points in the life rhythms which happen blatantly around us in temperate North America. Like the swelling of buds under the surging pressure of the trees' reactivated plumbing after the hard freezes stop. Like the fugue-like hooting of pairs of horned owls at rival pairs just before the territories are settled a little after Christmas-time and the woods fall silent while the great birds nest. Like the arrival of the whippoorwill. Like the noisy nuptial flights of the woodcock in February's icy dusk. Like the grand entrance of the whooping cranes at Arkansas, heralded and tallied in every newspaper in the country. Lamentably, the biotic milestones we mark during the year are usually annoyances rather than delights. We can hardly ignore the leaves to be raked into piles, the snow to be shoveled, the weeds to be pulled, the flies to be swatted. But let's not overlook the better that sweetens the bitter.

The annual life cycle has neither end nor beginning, so we must contrive a starting point. We will soar once around the sun through the biologic zodiac and meet the spring ephemerals at their moment of glory.

Among certain students of life, convention partitions the year into six periods rather than four. What we typically call spring is divided into two aspects of very different biological signifi- cance, as is winter. I have never seen a detailed explanation of precisely which events define the biochronal aspects of a year. Such a schedule must be approached one locality at a time. I will broadly sketch here the events associated with the aspects of the living year in the deciduous oak-hickory forests in which I live. I will offer no dates because the times vary grossly with latitude and altitude. Anyway, that's the whole point—marking time by events in nature, not by numbers on a piece of paper beneath a funeral home advertisement.

VERNAL: Spring in full swing. The leafbuds are open on the woody plants and within two or three weeks full foliage deploys. The trees produce most of their new wood in the initial rush of vernal growth. Birds immediately build their nests in the new foliage, lay and incubate. The bullthistle grows rapidly from the low rosette in which it endured winter. Fruit trees bloom, insects pollinate, young fruit sets. Tiny rabbits, newly weaned, struggle to burrow through the rank new grass beneath last year's dried tops. Birds complete the on-nest chores of their first brood and fledge the young. You see the families moving through their terri- tories, adults rushing to stuff the gullets of the young who squat, wings aquiver, in anticipation. Their food cries fill the air.

44

AESTIVAL: High summer. It contains the hottest months. Grasshoppers chew the grasses and leap into flights that always end with a crash. Monarch larvae munch milkweed in bloom. Countless other caterpillars eat gaps in the woodland foliage. Blackberries ripen. Maypops grow behind elaborate floral pinwheels of form and color along the passionflower vine. The food cries of young redtailed hawks pierce the afternoon closeness. Murderous thunderstorms dump young doves from their nests in the tallest oaks. Fireflies sparkle just above the grass at dusk; in the treetops at midnight. The nights are noisy with buzzing bullbats, rasping insects, barred owls and sleepless mockingbirds.

SEROTINAL: The closest entry in my dictionary is serotine—"late-developing." This season embraces the year's remaining warmth, augmented by the gratuitous balm of Indian summer. The deciduous leaves are tattered and leathery. A swirling horde of migrating bullbats fills the meadow one evening. Huge dragonflies hunt the middle altitudes between the bullbats and a layer of chimney-swifts at a hundred feet—it is a bad night for insects. The goldfinch bends to the thistledown. And dominant in your perceptions is yellow—evening primrose and many asters, including goldenrod, warm the failing summer with endless displays of yellow. Why, I ask the experts. Maybe pollinator preference. Nobody knows. Endless rivers of blackbirds commute from foraging grounds in cities and sprouting grainfields to roosting woodlots. The doves fledge their final (perhaps fifth) brood of the year. Acorns and hickory nuts and walnuts pepper the forest floor. Black gum and persimmon trees disrobe for the year; their ripe fruit dangle invitingly before bird and beast. Poke stems redden, clusters of the purple berries nourish early migrating birds. Just before dawn, the tremulous wail of the screech owl wafts eerily through the great oaks. In the wee hours of a late September morning, this tiny raptor once awakened me in my cabin, warbling the ominous delirium that somehow gladdens the forest. Soon the barred owl WHOOO-AAAWed its one-note threat, and a mile away a horned owl boomed her regal cadence through the serotinal Carolina predawn. I doubt another human heard those

45

three owls in concert, but I'll bet a lot of mice and voles took notice.

AUTUMNAL: Frost sharpens the sunrise and chlorophyl retires from the foliage, unmasking the yellow carotinoid pigments. The cold inhibits the flow of sugar from the leaves, causing spectacular red and purple anthocyanins to accumulate in the sumac tops and maple canopies. Life flows southward on a million wings, and the pokeberry clusters are soon stripped. Squirrels hustle through the woods, stopping on signal from their genes to bury the nut clenched in their teeth. Abscission membranes form at the end of leaf stems and cut off the plumbing. Autumnal gusts bluster about as if for no other purpose than to break the vascular bundles and scatter the leaves. A half-hour stroll through the woods and fields obliges you to spend equal time picking the beggars' lice, cockleburs, and Spanish needles from your clothes. These are animal-dispersed seeds and you are the dispersing animal. The pink globes on the strawberry bush open into five spherical segments with an orange berry dangling from each.

HIEMAL (or *Hibernal):* Cold. The boxturtle that buried itself in the cool mud of a streambank to escape the aestival heat now burrows into rotting vegetation to ward off the hibernal cold. It hibernates. So does the groundhog, its metabolic rate approaching zero. The skunk sleeps for days but emerges periodically to forage. Tracks of a gray fox quarter the snowy woods behind my house. I follow for miles and see two events written in the snow; a place where the little canid dug something from under a fallen log and another where it leaped six feet into the crotch of a tree, defecated, and resumed its trotting trek. The plumbing in the deciduous trees and shrubs is dormant, but next year's buds have already formed. They wait, compressed in an armor of scales. The massive bare arms of the oak creak under burdens of wind and ice. A friend and I watch a pair of squirrels spiral around the tree trunks and make unabashed love seventy-five feet up, the female clinging desperately to the underside of a branch, her suitor not giving a damn about the footing. The juices of the little blue berries on female cedar trees take on a woodsy-fresh smell. I love to

46

pinch and rub them on my face; and every now and then some-
body asks about the fantastic after-shave lotion I'm wearing. The
birds that pass the hiemal with us are principally seed-eaters
with stout, conical beaks: the Fringillidae—sparrows, finches,
cardinals, towhees. One among them is the snowbird, the very
symbol of winter. Its formal name: *Junco hiemalis.*

PREVERNAL: The days have been lengthening for some weeks.
But it is still very cold. The woodcock *PEENT*s his nasal love call
and warbles through his nuptial loops in the dusk. Spicebush and
jessamine bloom in defiance of the freezing nights. Male alder
flowers dangle in golden catkins over the stream; the slanting sun
electrifies the glowing female flowers like laser rubies. The horned
owls hatched a month ago. They peer cautiously over the nest
ledge as I approach, bobbing their heads from side to side in
order to perceive depth by motion parallax. Sap begins to flow in
the deciduous trees and shrubs. Dogwood and redbud bloom over
succulent morels. Leaf buds swell. But they don't open. Not yet.
They wait, as if for supreme approval, for a very special event to
take place on the forest floor.

That event is the appearance of the spring ephemeral wildflowers. I define spring ephemerals as those herbs of the deciduous forest floor which time their appearance carefully between
the end of the hard freezes and the closing of the forest canopy.
After the canopy erupts to seize the sunlight, the flowers set
seed, the foliage withers and dies, and no vestige of the plants is
visible above ground until the appointed prevernal moment a
year later. The precision of this timing can't be overstressed. If
the plants jump the gun by a fortnight, a late cold snap can wither
them or ground their insect pollinators. If they dally a week, they
may lose their moment in the sun to the spreading giants above.

In this brief span, between the numb of winter's cold and the
darkness of spring's shade, the spring ephemerals do their thing.
Their whole thing. They send their foliage up through the forest
litter. They photosynthesize a year's supply of food and store it
in an underground bulb or tuber. They flower, have their gene
pool refreshed by insects bearing pollen from other colonies of
their species, and make their seeds.

47

A trout lily thrusts its floral stem through the melting snow. (Though notably cold-tolerant, it and other spring ephemerals must time their emergence carefully between the end of the hard freezes and the closing of the deciduous canopy above.)

The ancestors of these plants might have chosen to live in some habitat other than mature hardwood forests. But having selected the deciduous woodlands, they had to find a way to get enough sunlight for growth and reproduction. The method they adopted was to fit their schedule carefully into that of the dominant hardwoods and make a grab for the prevernal sunlight. Their food-making machinery is geared entirely to full sunlight—such as it is at that time of year on the forest floor. The plants cannot function on the pittance of energy which filters to the ground through several stories of woody plant foliage. They don't even try. They simply photosynthesize furiously for their appointed two or three weeks, then die back to soil level, perhaps even before the canopy completely closes.

Ephemeralism is plant behavior characterized by brief moments of flower and leaf production separated by long latent periods spent either as seeds or underground storage organs. The ephemeral habit helps organisms avoid stress. Some animals even employ the device, usually to see them through such hard times as droughts of unpredictable length. Some fish and reptiles, for example, lay eggs which can last for years in the baked mud of arid lands until a sudden wet spell lets them hatch and quickly complete their reproductive cycle. Ephemeralism is common among desert plants which must spend long periods between rains as seeds. Other plants in other stress-laden habitats employ other versions of ephemeralism. We speak here of those few herbaceous plants which have adapted to life in deciduous forests by changing their schedule to fit that of the dominant hardwoods, and which spend most of the year below ground as a result.

This particular type of ephemeralism, this unique adjustment by a group of herbs to the growth patterns and timing cycles of other members of the plant community, suggests a long coexistence. Long enough to lead some who have studied the phenomenon to think of these communities as quasi-organisms—massive, complex alliances with inter-relationships between the species organized as highly as the organs of a single being.

Organisms in any community tend to be closely interlocked. They are not just *there;* they are there because of one another. Where the deciduous forests of North America constitute the

48

climax in the local succession of plants, the biotic community is spectacular in its relationships. These woods are diverse beyond comprehension, yet fiercely unified.

A century ago, the great American chestnut dominated the eastern deciduous forest, claiming half the canopy and sending down its mouth-watering mast by the ton. Then someone released a disease. It felled every chestnut on the continent. The priceless tree was gone: the street vendors in Manhattan never again to push the carts of roasted native nuts beneath the nostrils of Wall Street; the cherished wood now a relic on the floors of old Appalachian barns. Humanity lamented its own folly. But the forests? The oaks and hickories and poplars closed ranks. They forgot the wretched story, drew on the strength of their diversity and reconstituted the deciduous canopy. And today these deciduous stands are available to more Americans than are any other woodlands. The spring ephemerals, in their time and place, are unique expressions of the interlocking strength and beauty of the deciduous community.

It's risky business being a spring ephemeral, poking your tender nose up into what seems like the dead of winter. But it's a living. And that's all any organism asks of evolution. This strange habit has attracted members of several prominent herbaceous families with nothing more in common than a schedule and an organ for storing starch below ground. By my count there are five families represented. For the taxonomically inclined, they are the Brassicaceae (the turnip family), the Ranunculaceae (buttercup family), the Liliaceae (lily family) and the Fumariacae and the Portulacaceae (which don't have a common family name). I say it's my count because I've never seen an authoritative list of spring ephemerals. In fact there is precious little in the literature on the subject. The individual plants, of course, are all identified, described, studied, pressed, classified and dissected. But a puzzled squint is all I ever got out of a botanist when I asked for references on the spring ephemerals as a group or on their relationship with the rest of the forest.

Trout Lily. Usually the first of the true ephemerals to bloom and my favorite. It's tiny as lilies go. Perhaps six inches tall.

But it would take a dim-witted herb to wave two or three feet of soft greenery around in the freezing prevernal nights. It loves the moist bottomlands beneath the hackberry, ash and river birch and the low oaken slopes studded with beech.

I remember once finding a dragonfly entering adulthood on an ash tree just above a trout lily. The creature had crawled from its hunting grounds beneath the swirling rapids up a four-foot bank, trekked across ten feet of alluvium and climbed a foot up the ash. I'll never forget what time of year the big brown dragonfly with the green stripes does its metamorphosis. The trout lily won't let me.

There are other names for the plant—dogtooth violet, adder's tongue. Its formal name is *Erythronium americanum*. I first heard the name pronounced by a very proper British lady who stood erect and gestured with a little finger toward the *"EddiTHROWnyum."* The bladelike waxy leaves with their dreamy swirls of rust against the shiny green suggested the skin of the brown trout to early Americans. And some say the plant appears just as the trout begin to bite in the spring.

On each plant a single flower nods from a vertical stem. I have seen the flowers melt their way to sunlight through a light snow, releasing last year's energy to burn a neat opening. The closed sepals of the new flowers are a liverish mauve in color. The sepals later curl upward to display a bright yellow underside matching the petals. The anthers are pale when first displayed, then brighten to almost the same ruby iridescence of the female tag alder flower.

The pollinators can't resist. The trout lily is among the honey

Toothwort and trout lily bloom at the base of an oak, before its leaves close a canopy above.

bee's first conquests of the year. There is also a little green-bodied bee, a third the honey bee's size, that burrows adroitly among the sexual parts and emerges sparkling with pollen. Tiny black ants move like punctuation marks over the poetry of the little lily's floral curves. A generality I draw about the spring ephemerals' hearty pollinators is that I find them only on specific prevernal flowers; except for the honey bee, I never see any of them during the rest of the year. No self-respecting scientist would draw this inference on so little "data," but, in the recesses of my amateurish mind, I see a specialization of these insects upon the spring ephemerals, consistent with the deciduous woodlands' motif of coordinated kinships.

I take a parochial view of *Erythronium* because I see only one species where I live. The genus is actually cosmopolitan, reaching its densest distribution in the Pacific Northwest. *Erythronium montanum* and *Erythronium grandiflorum,* the avalanche and glacier lilies, respectively, are said to be spectacular punching up through the rapidly retreating snow to bloom within hours after the melt. They ornament the slopes of the Rocky and Cascade ranges in aspen groves and open parkland. Their appearance is triggered by the same stimulus which summons the trout lily in the east—the end of the ice and snow. But on the parklands and subalpine cirques, crowding from taller herbs rather than the closing of a deciduous canopy forces the western *Erythroniums* to retreat below ground after a few days in the sun.

"ClitOONyah," announced the very British voice, triumphantly. "*Claytonia caroliniana,*" I confirmed in my Justice and Bell *Wildflowers of North Carolina.* There's a more northern species, *Claytonia virginica,* with more narrow leaves, which I see in Pennsylvania and in the Appalachians. Actually they both occupy vast ranges east of the prairies and are everywhere known affectionately as "spring beauty." *Claytonia lanceolata* is their counterpart in the Rockies.

Spring beauty is predominantly white. Its five petals blush with varying intensities of an outrageous magenta pink. Tiny gnatlike pollinators waddle among the sexual parts, reflecting the erotic hues in their glassy wings. Successive flowers unfold —one each day—from a fiddlehead of buds on the spring beauty.

A half-dozen or more blossoms cycle through the reproductive act, one after another, to hedge the devastation of an errant cold snap. The later flowers always seem to me the pinkest. By "later" I mean those opening a week or ten days after the first blossoms. The whole of spring beauty's foliation and blooming can span as little as two weeks.

Euell Gibbons devotes great passages to the harvest of the tiny tubers in which the spring beauty stores its starch. A judicious thinning does them no harm, according to the master forager. Baked in the coals of a campfire with the day's catch of trout, spring beauty's little potatoes are said to be among life's great gustatory rewards. I have frankly never found spring beauty in such numbers that I would feel comfortable digging them up, but Gibbons's mention of their harvestability (and numbers) introduces an important point about spring ephemerals, collectively. They are usually found in colonies, because many of them reproduce vegetatively from a spreading root system. Beginning with a single sexually reproduced seed, a clone of these plants radiates outward at a constant annual rate, thus enabling botanists to age the colonies. One clone of trout lilies in Wisconsin was found by this method to be three hundred fourteen years old.

I know a place in the woods where a stunted holly clings to a salient of soil bulging from a streambank. The stream has decided that it shall occupy the holly's cubic year of earth and patiently, inexorably, it is undermining the tree. In the four years I have watched, the stream has tunneled under the holly until its ball of soil hangs corbeled precariously over the current. Each freshet, I always fear, will be the holly's last. It will be a shame when the little tree goes, because at its base grows a colony of wood anemone.

And wood anemone in my neck of the woods is not plentiful. I live at the southern edge of its range. The colony under the holly sends up the whitest flowers imaginable, yet on the other side of the stream another clone blooms with touches of rust and purple diffused through the sepals.

The wood anemone (Anemone quinquefolia) seems as particular about the time of day it opens its flowers as about the time of

*Along moist deciduous
bottomlands, colonies of
Dutchman's breeches
"clone" radially from a
sexually reproduced
plant.*

year it erupts. The closed flowers follow the prevernal sun
through its southerly arc, opening only for a little while at mid-
day. If it is sunny. Perhaps it is only then that the anemone's
pollinators are about; perhaps it is only then that the little ephemerals wish to be visited. Whichever, the flowers pass most of the
day with their sepals (the anemone has no petals) folded modestly
forward around their yellow sexual parts.

Gratuitous pedantry, that's what I called it. Although I may
have deserved it. I was picking the brain of a botanist friend,
asking if *Corydalis* (which I pronounced as if it rhymed with
"borealis") were a spring ephemeral.

"Cor-ry-DAL-is?" he said quizzically. "Corydalis? I don't believe I . . . oh, yes, yes, CoRIDalis."

Anyway, it is an ephemeral and this is how its name is written
—*Corydalis aurea*. Golden corydalis. It sends up masses of fern-
like foliage sprinkled with tiny yellow flowers. It is in the family
Fumariaceae, a prominent ephemeral clan which includes the
Dutchman's breeches and squirrel corn. The golden corydalis
has two congeners which are spring ephemerals and one, *Corydalis sempervirens*, which is definitely not. The latter's name is
apt; it means "everliving"—not dying back to the ground after
a brief period of foliage and flower. But Corydalis species, uniquely among the spring ephemerals, carry the adaptation another
step. They do not have a storage organ; they do not reproduce
vegetatively; they are not perennials. The whole plant dies in the
vernal darkness. Corydalis survive the fifty dormant weeks as
seeds. So you won't necessarily find them in the same spot
next year. But they'll likely be close by.

Dutchman's breeches—and squirrel corn, its look-alike of the
higher elevations and latitudes—are strongly ephemeral. And
beautiful. If you line up the blossoms with the sun properly, they
glow like lightbulbs; they are three dimensional and not, like
most flowers, flat. Look for both on steep wooded slopes under
beech and maple and tulip poplar. Their genus is *Dicentra*. They
have a congener, *Dicentra eximia*, commonly called bleeding
heart, which is emphatically not an ephemeral. You can find it in

54

full bloom and foliage from May to November (that is, from the late prevernal through the autumnal).

The turnip family contributes at least one spring ephemeral to the woodlands. Toothwort; *Dentaria laciniata*. I often see it blooming slightly upslope from a spring beauty. *And* sharing a pollinator with that ephemeral—a squat, fuzzy little fly that looks like a bee and hovers before the blossoms, probing the nectaries with dark, needle-like mouth parts. I know there are many species of bee flies, but the only one I have so far been privileged to meet is the fat little fuzzball who visits the toothwort and the spring beauty.

The Eno River flows near my home in the Piedmont region of North Carolina. There is a spot where the river reflects off an ancient granite mass for a mile or two. The waters edge against the granite scarp, passing beneath bare stony ledges alternating with steep wooded slopes. Along the Eno's edge and up these slopes grows the greatest collection of spring ephemerals I have ever seen. Except for squirrel corn, which is a mountain plant, every eastern ephemeral mentioned so far grows here. Plus a bonus—the false rue anemone (*Isopyrum biternatum*) which I have found nowhere else.

I don't know that this plant is rare, but it's probably not taking over the world, either. I'm happy knowing of one little colony growing beside a boulder covered with mosses and walking fern. You could cover the clone with your coat. The lovely little white-flowered herbs huddle together for what seems like only a moment. The trout lily and spring beauty bloom for comparatively long periods before and after the *Isopyrum*. I doubt that the clone sees the light of day for a full fortnight.

Most of the true spring ephemerals can be considered common, even abundant, but don't bother looking for them in a pine forest or a marsh or an open field. Find a stand of oaks and hickories and stake it out for exploration. At the appointed time, the slopes and moist bottoms of nearly every deciduous woodlot in eastern North America gleam with colonies of spring ephemerals. You don't really have to look for them. Just go into the prevernal woods and the ephemerals will find you. They will glare at you as beacons through the open woodlands—throbbing riots of

Spring ephemeralism is a stress-avoidance method employed by members of several prominent herbaceous families. The toothwort (Dentaria laciniata shown here with syrphid fly pollinator) is in the turnip family.

whites and yellows dancing in the leaves, spilling over rocks and hosting throngs of noisy pollinators.

Accept no substitutes. The woods are full of other herbs in bloom along with the true ephemerals. Bloodroot, windflower,

57

hepatica, jack-in-the-pulpit, mayapple, chickweed and the trilliums all bloom with the ephemerals, but they differ in one major respect—their foliage persists after the canopy closes. These herbs are worthy and beautiful in their own right, but they have an entirely different solution to the problem of getting enough sunlight on the forest floor. They are equipped with a highly efficient brand of chlorophyl which can continue food production in the weak light (sometimes only a hundredth the intensity of direct sunlight) filtering down to ground level. These plants are true shade plants, not true ephemerals.

If the literature on spring ephemerals is sketchy, that only lends significance to your own observations. Besides, the place for discovery of this sort is not in a book or musty herbarium, but on the wooded slopes of your neighborhood. Your appointment is set for the day the leaf buds begin to open on the trees.

4 / *Plant Succession*

Long AGO, we are told, the earth was covered by a mantle of newly cooled lava devoid of life. Somehow, through a process we can almost understand yet scarcely believe, life developed and spread across the whole earth. The first life forms were simple; but over unutterable spans of time they altered the soil and atmosphere, paving the way for more advanced forms until ultimately whole forests stood, with their attendant fauna, where once only a green ooze had shimmered in the lava pocks.

Altered the soil and atmosphere. The egregiousness of this understatement offends our appreciation of life. Of plants especially.

Wait, you say. I love plants. I tend my flowers, I clip my hedge. I even grow my own tomatoes in the summer. I have heard the evening wind in the pines. The prevernal elan of the daffodils gladdens me as much as anyone. I need no lecture on appreciating plants.

Fine.

Then let's say this note deals with veneration rather than appreciation. We know what plants do and we appreciate them for it. We get into veneration when we think about what plants were and what they have done.

Back to the newly cooled lava. Imagine the great caller of the cosmic shots standing astride a mound of hardened magma, beaming with satisfaction at the newly created firmament and picturing in his or her mind's eye the birds and beasts to be set loose in the gardens which will grow there.

You no doubt notice a lack of originality. Correctly so. Hardly a human culture has flourished that didn't deal with life's origins by some variation of this scenario. However, a half-dozen super-geniuses and ten thousand tireless researchers have, in the last century, put us in position to note the impossibility of spontaneously populating a planet with higher life forms. Everyone now knows that the form of life must flow with glacial slowness from simple to complex.

Notice that I boldly presume not the improbability but the *impossibility* of abruptly populating the bare earth with animals. True, they wouldn't have anything to eat, but hunger would not have a chance to overtake them. About three breaths of the earth's precambrian atmosphere of methane and carbon dioxide would be all they could endure. So there is a basic aspect to the evolution of life on earth which is often obscured by the fancy stuff we hear about dinosaurs, archeopterixes and prehumans. No such critters would ever have come into existence if plants hadn't first given them a breathable atmosphere. Here are the facts:

The plants inherited an atmosphere devoid of free oxygen.

The plants took oxygen out of the primordial earth's original complement of minerals and atmospheric gases and released it, free and uncombined.

As a result, the "air" is now twenty percent oxygen.

No animal can live without oxygen to breathe.

That's why I think it's a dangerous understatement to say that the simpler life forms, mostly plants, altered the soil and atmosphere. In terms of what it takes to sustain modern life, they *created* the soil and atmosphere.

They are still doing it.

The atmosphere, thanks to the green plants, is now 79 percent nitrogen, 20 percent oxygen and 1 percent other gases, including CO_2, a principal product of animal breathing and other organic combustion. If a lone chemical reaction were to be singled out as the one most important to life on earth, it would be

$$H_2O + CO_2 \xrightarrow{\text{sunlight}} glucose + O_2$$

60

This is the formula for plant photosynthesis. Without this basic miracle, none of life's other thousands of reactions could occur. In this heroic act, green plants stir in a few simple ingredients like water, carbon dioxide, and solar energy to produce for animals all the food they eat and all the oxygen they breathe.

Science calculates that the earth's combustion rate—principally, the respiration of animals, the rapid burning of plant material (fire) and the slow burning of plant material (rot)—uses all the atmosphere's free oxygen every two thousand years. The plants, of course, continuously replace the used oxygen.

This does not by any stretch of the imagination mean that we have a two thousand year supply of oxygen floating around us or that, if plant life were extirpated today, it would take that long for us to choke. Within a very few years the animals in a plant-less world would reduce the air's oxygen content below the levels they need to breathe; the choking would start almost immediately. Especially so, given the rate at which western man gobbles oxygen to burn fossil fuels to power his industries and keep the temperature immediately around his body at exactly 72° Fahrenheit. (The human body, by the way, is perfectly capable of functioning through a temperature range well wider than a hundred Fahrenheit degrees, a genetic endowment which we seem intent on losing.)

I was once at a cocktail party given in Washington for officers and leading members of the Ecological Society of America. Finding myself in a room which contained more knowledge on life's interrelationships than perhaps any other on earth at the moment, I listened intently to the conversation around me. A little knot of the great scientists was clustered in animated debate, jabbing with pipe stems at one another's rumpled tweeds. One of the "majors" had just started shipping a petrochemical herbicide in super-tankers. The ecologists, in their carefully measured tones of understatement, were debating how long it would take for a film of this herbicide spreading over the seas after a Torrey Canyon-style shipwreck to kill enough phytoplankton to reduce the supply of atmospheric oxygen to a fatal level (seventy percent of our oxygen is produced by sea plants.) Ten to twenty years was the consensus.

Tidbits like that help me appreciate plants. What they have done and are doing for the atmosphere is of the most immediate importance to us. What they do for the soil is more subtle, but no less important, and certainly no less worthy of our awareness than the atmospheric contribution.

The soil.

Back again to the newly cooled lava. And to the still-uncomprehended origin of life. All we know is that some chemicals got together into the basic life unit we call the cell and that solar energy made the cells go. By another mystifying leap the cells eventually began to differentiate into specialized plant tissue. The higher plants eventually came into being, and they began to radiate adaptively into new niches. Before the early plants ever left the water they had probably changed the atmosphere radically. By and by, they ventured onto the lava. Their roots began to grind it to rubble. Their rotting litter mixed with the minerals to form the primordial soils. The great work continued, snowballing in mass and velocity. Over the eons one type of vegetation succeeded another, each benefiting from conditions created by its predecessors.

Today, in much less than a human lifespan, an analogous process of plant succession can be observed all around us. With life forms already in existence, with seeds lying dormant in the soil and spores already in the air, the pace of plant succession can be very rapid. It is conceivable that a man could watch a bare rock face disappear in his lifetime under the compost of successive plant types as lichens yield to moss, moss to herbs and herbs to woody plants.

Plant succession is best explained in terms of its end result—climax. In a climax condition the climate, soil and many other factors dictate a dominant vegetation which replaces itself with its own offspring. The climax plant community is stable and, barring catastrophe, changes only over geologic time. Any disruptive force such as wind, blight, fire or human intervention opens opportunities for "pioneer" plants. The pioneers do not replace themselves with their own kind but create the conditions their successors need. After a disturbance, one type of pioneer vegetation follows another until the climax equilibrium is restored.

Lyndon Johnson used to ask his aides after lengthy factual briefings, "Therefore what?" Well, therefore, any plot of land, be it a freshly worked roadbed, a fallow field, a vacant lot or your front lawn will, if left alone, host a reasonably predictable series of plant types which will ultimately stabilize in a permanent climax. The associated birds, mammals and insects will undergo comparable transitions because they depend on the plants. Since most of the territory in temperate North America has been disturbed by human intervention, without recognizing the phenomenon of plant succession, we cannot understand the natural forces at work on our land, let alone manage our environment. It is, alas, a process so complex that, without devoting a lifetime to its study, we can discuss it only by gross simplification.

Biologists speak of two types of plant succession—primary, where plants move onto barren surfaces; and secondary, which occurs after an established plant community has been disturbed. Primary succession builds soil; secondary succession holds it in place. Erosion is the common enemy of both, but except in the severest circumstances, the plants eventually prevail and cover every surface with a mixture of their decomposed remains and the mineral rubble of the substrate.

Lichens are the initial agents of primary succession. They are very old and primitive plants, but time has not changed their basic function. They carry the pioneering vanguard onto barren surfaces.

A lichen is an alliance between an alga and a fungus. A very close alliance. Their life cycles are meshed and interdependent to the point that they are, in appearance and function, a single plant. Together they take a wedded name apart from either component. Algae and fungi which live together as lichens are almost never found living separately.

The alga contains chlorophyl enabling it to manufacture carbohydrates, some of which are used by the fungus. It is thought that the fungus produces acids which dissolve rock-bound minerals used by the alga. This chemical action works to decompose the lithic mass and bring it into the biotic flow. The rock is also subjected to lichen-powered mechanical forces. Water seeps into the acid-etched crevices in the rock beneath the lichens. It freezes, expands, flakes off and pulverizes bits of rock. On a huge granite outcrop in South Carolina I have seen blade-thin shards piled at the base of the rounded monoliths, often still wearing the colorful splashes of lichen which chiseled them from the mother stone. Stone Mountain, near Atlanta, is a nationally prominent example of a site where lichen power is at work on the first step of primary succession. This same process is visible on rocks, and sometimes even on buildings, within yards of your home.

After pulverizing the rocky materials, lichens advance the succession process another step. The powdered minerals mix with organic debris which collects on the rough surfaces of lichens adhering to rocks. The spores of ferns and mosses and the seeds of flowering plants germinate on these deposits, gnaw at the underlying rock with their roots and add clout to the forces of rock decomposition. The plants die and add their detritus to the collection. Gradually the soil pockets spread and deepen; irresistibly, the stony surfaces are infected with life.

Primary succession is not limited to theaters of struggle on bare rock. Erosion and human enterprise, sometimes independently but often in devastating collusion, can strip the life from a softer surface. Sands or clays or lifeless muck then lie prostrate before the ravages of ice, wind and water. Sometimes these erosive forces must act, for a time, to smooth out the contours and gentle the slopes before life can gain a purchase. But sooner or later the scars blush red with little regiments of British Soldiers, a lichen of the bare open spaces, holding the line against erosion. Green and brown lichens, which look like stacked golf tees, seem to grow up through or on older stands of British Soldiers. These lichens sift the chaff from the winds and the organic collections begin. It's only a matter of time until conditions will support the flowering plants—and the seeds are forever on the breast of the wind and in the bowels of the birds.

Once an area has acquired a mantle of soil, the forces of secondary succession move to establish the climax vegetation. And if the climax is ever disrupted, to restore it.

Climax vegetation differs from place to place. If you live in the Rockies, the climax may be groves of aspen or conifers or, at higher elevations, alpine tundra. The climax in the Great Plains

—the prairie—is so battered that you can find only tiny remnants that have somehow been spared the gang plows. This prairie climax—thousands of square miles of grasslands—once supported herds of ungulates to rival those on the veldts of Africa. Conjuring a vista of these endless, hugely productive grasslands is a reverie trip well worth taking. It further saddens Aldo Leopold's lament that the *Silphium* will never again tickle the bellies of the bison on the wild prairies.

To the north, the boreal coniferous forests lie in a great band across the continent and, more northerly still, the arctic tundra vegetation of stunted willows forms the climax dominant. Heading south from eastern Canada, the climax shifts to maple-birch, then into the vast broadleaf deciduous stands of the Appalachians and the Mississippi valley. On the eastern coastal plain, from New Jersey to the Gulf Coast, the southern coniferous forests form the climax stands.

The climax vegetation is always associated with the fauna of that region. Geographic masses which are unified by a given formation of climax plant and animal life are called "biomes." The vegetative types just mentioned lend their names to such major North American biomes as desert, grassland, tundra, northern and southern coniferous, and eastern deciduous.

Secondary succession is constantly at work in all these biomes, moving the vegetative mix inexorably back toward the climax after any disturbance. The precision and predictability of the succession steps makes an overview of this phenomenon one of the most clarifying insights a naturalist can acquire about the biome he lives in.

I am most familiar with the eastern deciduous biome because I have never lived for any length of time in another. I hope to do something about that someday, but for the moment I must approach plant succession from a Piedmont parochialism. Besides, I am a mite apprehensive about getting to know another biome intimately. I'm not sure I could stand the excitement.

So let's take a look at secondary succession in the hardwood forests which still grace the rolling uplands of much of the eastern United States. Most of this lush broadleaf acreage has been cut over, farmed, grazed and grubbed, at some point in the past two hundred years. But less of it is in cultivation now than, say, seventy-five years ago. There is incredibly little of this five-million-acre woodlot in its maiden condition. (Joyce Kilmer Wilderness Area in the Carolina-Tennessee Highlands.) A further precious increment has returned to climax after some form of molestation. But a vast acreage is somewhere along the march between rape and recovery. Virtually anytime you glance out your car window along a highway in the east, you see land (if it's not under immediate cultivation) cloaked in some form of secondary succession verdure.

In the eastern deciduous biome the climax vegetation consists of mixed stands of oak, hickory, (tulip) poplar (which isn't really a poplar) and, until recently, chestnut. Huge trees. Two or three people could scarcely link arms around them. The crowns of the poplars have been known to reach altitudes of two hundred feet. With the oaks and hickories, they close a tight canopy over several clearly defined subdominant levels down to the fungal mycelia in the leaf litter. Each level has characteristic members, both plant and animal. I propose we take a few hundred years and construct a climax deciduous forest.

Let's say you live in a Philadelphia suburb. If you stop mowing your lawn today your great-great-grandchildren would inherit a maturing grove of nut-bearing hardwoods. In the meantime you and your descendants would see the lot move through a loosely predictable sequence of greenery, not all of which would delight your neighbors. Suppose that in the summer of 1976 a mishap sets into motion the following sequence:

July 4: A parade led by a marching band wends its way down the street past your house, celebrating the nation's bicentennial. You are doing your yard work. The twirling of batons and the dazzle of the Shriner's motorcycle escort divert your attention. You cut off your toe with the walkway edge trimmer.

July 11: A week has passed; the grass needs cutting again. But you're still on crutches and, anyway, the contemplation of your remaining toes sticking out of the cast has eroded your commitment to the maintenance of a sterile, manicured monoculture lawn as a means of expressing civic virtue. Maybe you'll just let nature take its course and see what happens.

Labor Day: The fescue and clover you planted and lavishly subsidized over the years is waist-high and vigorously producing seed. A few Queen Anne's lace gently nod their white umbels in the dog-days sun. Fireflies rest during the day on the underside of the umbels; some die and leave their corpses clinging. Honey bees shuttle between dandelion flowers on foot-high stems. Your persistence has reduced the neighborhood Property Values Committee campaign to bring you back into the fold, which began with missionary zeal, to a few half-hearted obscene phone calls

In "old field" succession over much of North America, the second summer of abandonment is given over to the asters. Here a red admiral lends his colors to a late-summer collection of dogbane asters.

daily. A black rat snake has taken up residence to hunt the meadow mice, striking them in their tunnels in the grassy tussocks. Rabbits play in the headlights when you come home at night.

January, 1977: The tall grasses of late summer lie in a brown, ankle-deep mat. Some winter annuals are visible. Little green circles of horseweed freshen between the grass clumps. The flattened rosette of a thistle spreads over the rusting blade of the edge trimmer and onto the shrinking walkway. White-throated sparrows and cardinals and towhees and juncos forage for grass seeds.

Summer, 1977: Your grasses come on strong again, but they are not alone. Weeds of many types begin their struggle with your artificial grass community. Crabgrass crowds it mercilessly. The thistle rears its pink torches in dominance. It's branches hum with industry. Sorrel, plantain, woolly mullein and foxtail grass muscle in. Birds foraging in the weeds drop blackberry and poke seeds which germinate and grow conservatively that first full summer of abandonment. Toward late summer the horseweed begins to dominate the struggle. A meadowlark has seen your grassy island from afar and arrives to announce his possession from your walkway lamp post.

Summer, 1978: This is the year of the asters. Several varieties are chest high by midsummer, bearing small white flowers in profusion at all levels. Pollinators race between them in frantic quest of nectar. The thistles, berry briars, poke and mullein are headhigh by June. The late aestival winds bring migrating monarchs to the asters of Indian summer. When your lot browns in autumn, the sunlight catches the downy seed plumes of a few broomsedges.

1979: The broomsedge takes over. It muscles out the asters, poke, briars and thistles, and forms a golden brown blanket over your premises, thinning the ground cover. These are the conditions pine seeds need to germinate, and so in fall you notice a few pine seedlings peeping between the broomsedge clumps. Some cedars also appear.

1980: The pines and cedars reach above the broomsedge and remaining briars. A point of clarification about the role of the eastern red cedar (*Juniperus virginiana*) in deciduous succession

—it has none. The cedar grows in virtually every eastern habitat, from the barrier island sand dunes on the Atlantic Coast to the western plains. It grows in all succession stages in its range.

1990: Your lawn is now a dense stand of young evergreens fifteen feet tall. They completely dominate and shade the available growing space. A mat of dried pine needles covers the ground, decomposing slowly and raising the soil acidity to levels too hostile for most other plants. For ten or fifteen years the pines may be just about the sole occupants of your "lawn." Except for the warblers and squirrels and bluejays and nuthatches. The arrival of these woods creatures marks the end of open space and the beginning of woodlands. But succession is nowhere near finished with your property.

2010: The pines, maturing, tower forty feet above your house. The understory is more open now because the pines have shed their lower limbs as they competed vertically for sunlight. The upper story is a solid canopy of evergreen boughs fecund with seed-bearing cones. The pines have no offspring below them, however, for it is still too dark there for their seedlings to survive. But maple and poplar and sweet gum seedlings are more tolerant of the darkness. They establish an understory which provides food and cover for new forms of wildlife and assures the eventual doom of the pine forest. In the pine crowns you notice collections of twigs and sticks—the nesting platforms of jays and crows. If your lot were contiguous with a few hundred others, you might at this stage begin to see evidence of deer browsing on the young deciduous saplings. Foxes would no doubt have found hunting ground and refuge there, sharing with the barred owl the bounteous populations of pine vole which have replaced the meadow mouse as principal rodent on your tract.

The pines thin themselves as they mature. Individuals succumb with strange quickness to disease or disadvantage, dying in July, perhaps, after growing vigorously in May. Rot is equally rapid. Insects and fungi attack as soon as the needles begin to brown. And so your lot begins to attract some woodpeckers. Smaller ones at first, like the downy and the hairy, hammer at the dead pine trunks to get the larvae of the woodborers. If you want to salvage a pine for firewood, get it before all the needles fall.

Ultimately an abandoned field or backyard in the eastern deciduous biome will stabilize under a climax canopy of oaks and hickories.

A sub-dominant level of dogwood, redbud and sourwood occupy the middle story between the oaken canopy and the shrub layer.

A few months' delay and the adolescent life systems in your miniforest will have fueled their own fires with your standing sticks of solar energy.

The pines that survive dust your doorstep each spring with pollen. They grow fat cones filled with seeds. The cones open later in the year and birds and breezes take the seeds to germinate in the broomsedge patches of your neighbors who, noting your enjoyment of the succession drama, want to get in on the action.

2020: Toward autumn you see colorful displays of maple, sweet gum and tulip poplar saplings ranging upward between the venerable pine trunks, aiming at breaks in the canopy. The deciduous pioneers approach sexual maturity. The maples display their bee-wing seed samaras in spring. In autumn, purple finches, goldfinches and evening grosbeaks hang on the geodesic seed globes of the sweet gum. Squirrels shell the seeds from the artichoke-like structures on the tulip trees. The forest floor, still carpeted with pine needles, is richer now in herbaceous plants and deciduous seedlings. The nonconifers add their litter to the pine straw, sweetening the once-acid humus. There are many young plants now under the pine canopy, but none are pines.

2040: The few pines remaining stand like sentinels among their deciduous successors. The poplars, maples and sweet gums, maturing, dominate large areas of the canopy. Young oaks and hickories and beeches move into the new vacancies left by the retiring maples. You (or your successor) now mark the impact of the forest fauna on this phase of succession. The pines and maples and poplars can disperse their seeds almost entirely by

wind. Sweet gums utilize wind and, to a lesser extent, birds. But while pines still stand in a principally deciduous woods (signifying the newness of the hardwoods), every oak and hickory you see was probably planted by a squirrel. Later, when the oaks and hickories mature, they can reseed themselves simply by letting their mast fall to the ground. But wind doesn't carry acorns and hickory nuts very far, so the pioneer oaks and hickories in an area must be planted by squirrels.

2076: By the centennial summer of your lost toe, the process is nearly complete. A maturing, permanent woodlot of gnarled and shaggy hardwoods sends down its mast each fall where once you labored after your sputtering mower. As old oaks and hickories die, young oaks and hickories take their places. And the squirrels begin to export acorns to your neighbors' sweet gum woodlots. In return, the higher hardwood branches clutch the wads of sticks and leaves which are home to squirrel families. Cooper's hawks and horned owls sometimes commandeer these nests, reinforce them with more sticks, and raise young raptors to cull the sick and inept from among the birds and rodents of the forest.

Beneath the oaken canopy, which may always contain some tulip poplars, a subdominant story of dogwood, redbud, mulberry, sourwood and sassafras trees develops. These trees are adapted to living in the shade of the dominants. Even if an opening occurs in the canopy, they usually confine their crowns to a level below the first branches of the oaks and hickories.

Lower still is a layer of shrubs, short (one to ten feet) woody plants with several stems—*viburnum, vaccinium* (the blueberry genus), spicebush, and in the wetter, lower places, hazelnut and tag alder.

And finally, in a cool and dimly lit fairyland uniquely theirs, dwell the herbs and fungi of the forest floor. Around your great-grandson's feet grow the ferns, the woodland orchids (oh yes, orchids; a half-dozen types are common and plentiful beneath the hardwoods), the spring ephemerals in their time, the morels and a thousand other mushrooms in theirs. Lilies, wild ginger, wintergreen, false foxglove (parasitic on the roots of oak), beech drops (parasitic on the roots of beech), true and false Solomon's-seal, hepatica and chrysognomum make the hardwood floor a

Beneath the shrubs dwell the herbaceous plants adapted to life on the floor of a matured deciduous forest. This is Indian pipe, Monotropa uniflora, *an herb which needs no chlorophyl because its food comes from decaying forest-floor litter.*

Blueberries, along with other members of the genus Vaccinium *and with the opposite-leaved viburnums form a shrub layer.*

sacred garden for the lad. If your great-great-grandfather had stood in the same spot, he would have seen essentially the same vegetation. Although in his time the whole arrangement would have been virgin. The trees would have been bigger and the community, with the chestnuts in place, more diverse.

With at least four vegetative levels above ground, there are, as you would imagine, animals who specialize in each layer. And some who are at ease in several or all. The golden-crowned kinglet picks tiny insects from the two top layers, the ruby-crowned from the lower two. The woodhawks (Cooper's and sharp-shins) prey on them both and on all the other birds from the canopy to the leaf litter. More than a score of dendroid warblers nest at their particular levels in the hardwoods. Pileated and red-headed woodpeckers hammer in the highest boughs; the flicker picks in the leaf litter, the white marking above its tail arcing upward like a thrown snowball as you approach.

73

The specialization, the interlocking of lives, the continuous circuitry of energy and protoplasm in the climax deciduous forest demands, as strongly as it defies, appreciation. It is one of the richest and most magnificent of earthly collusions. And in a paltry two centuries, the forces of secondary succession restore it, regardless (almost) of the initial damage.

There is no way to tell precisely what route your freehold would take on its march back to the primordial. It may skip some of these steps; it may dwell on some for long periods; or it may add steps I could not think to mention. I have described what is called "old field" succession, that secondary process which takes a fallow field back to the native climax. Events in your lot may differ widely from classical old field succession, especially if the care and chemistry you applied to your lawn grossly altered the starting point. Or, as is more often the case, if the developer who built your subdivision denuded the site of all topsoil and vegetation for his greater convenience during construction— and for your greater heating and cooling bills thereafter.

Therefore what? Therefore man must labor ceaselessly against the tide of plant succession to make the land grow vegetation which is not part of the natural sequence. The climax condition emphasizes stability over productivity; so if you are trying to grow corn or pine pulpwood, you must arrest the succession process, create an unstable monoculture soaked in pesticides and energy subsidies borrowed from fossil fuels, and then hope for the best. Knowing of plant succession, we wonder why man alone struggles against it for his food and fiber while less clever creatures manage admirably by letting it work for them.

5 / *Deadwood*

THERE IS A POINT we might have added to those which differentiate a mature deciduous forest from the pine woods which precede it in succession. Hardwoods resist decay and the climax deciduous is rich in standing deadwood. Dead oak branches, even whole trees, stand for years after their juices cease to flow. While pine quickly rots and falls, the hardwoods, oak especially, fall—then rot. Slowly.

Standing deadwood is critically important to a living forest. The bare snags, branches and trunks serve forest animals—as hunting perches, dens for raising families and hibernating, nurseries for edible insects, sanctuaries from storm and from predator attack. Without deadwood, life would be hard, if not impossible, for many of the creatures who play in the forest concert.

I'd like to share with you an experience by which the value of deadwood gradually came into my awareness.

Several years ago I lived in College Park, Maryland, along Old Route 1, once the principal road linking Baltimore and Washington. The neighborhood had once been more elegant, less crowded than when I knew it. The nice old frame homes with spacious yards and gardens had been chewed into little chain-link lots, with identical "ranchettes" exactly forty feet from the street, exactly twenty feet apart. Route 1 was lined with commerce—some of it frankly tawdry.

One Sunday I set out to explore the woods whose crown rises for half a mile above the narrow commercial strip, built on fill on the west side of the highway. Past the drive-in liquor store I walked, past the "launderette," past Marge's Massage Parlor and Dance Studio, past the drive-in car wash, past an emporium which sold "gifts, curios, film, antiques and hams" to passers-by (through a drive-in window). I left the highway and walked through a vacant lot, freshly filled to the level of the highway, on which the only structure was the sign of a realtor offering to build, sell or lease at the pleasure of the tenant. At the back of the lot, I stood at the edge of a man-made precipice fifty feet above the tree stumps, automobile hulks and refrigerator carcasses protruding from the base of the fill.

It was winter—early March. At eye level were the crowns of some sourwoods. Above towered the tops of a tulip poplar and hickory overstory. Some of the trees were dead because the fill had engulfed their bases. Still, it was clear that I stood at the edge of a mature deciduous woodlot which encompassed a brisk stream and its adjoining lowlands. Not a large woodlot. Through the hiemal-bare branches I could see the limits of the woods on all sides: to the north bordered by the beltway, and to the west and south by the University of Maryland's golf course. Thirty acres, I estimated. The fact that most of the woods was low and moist seemed adequately to account for its existence. The better-drained elevations all around had long since found the nobler utilizations mentioned above.

I have included this detail to underscore the surroundings of the woodlot I was poised to enter. Suburban civilization, whether you love or loathe it, had effectively isolated this little deciduous community with the clear intent of eventually doing it in.

I found that the woodlot was incredibly rich in wildlife, almost as if it had been part of a vast primordial continuum rather than a shrinking little nest of wild existence. There were woodcocks, skunks, raccoons, opossums, rabbits and foxes. There were Cooper's hawks and red-shouldered hawks. There were downy woodpeckers, red-headed and red-bellied woodpeckers. There were even pileated woodpeckers. In the sloughs and on the stream there were mallards, teal, mergansers and wood ducks. And in a huge, dead tulip poplar, on a ledge left thirty feet up when one fork of the trunk broke away, there was a nest of great horned owls.

Standing deadwood provides nesting and roosting shelter for many forest animals. This pair of infant horned owls occupies a nest ledge in a dead poplar in a small woodlot.

I was flabbergasted.

I realized I could not plan on finding another horned owl nest. Ever. So I observed and photographed the birds as much as I could for as long as the young stayed in the dead poplar, and for a week or two after they fledged.

77

Here's the point. I was homesick, displaced to the city and constantly thirsty for the slightest expression of nature to brighten a lifestyle which, to me, had quickly become oppressive and demeaning. The owl nest was a windfall. Here was the most powerful bird of prey left in that part of the world—the eagles, rest their souls, have long since been exterminated. For weeks I did little and thought of nothing else. I watched them at dawn, at dusk and at every possible moment in between. Had I their light-gathering power, I would have watched them at night. But strangely, as the weeks passed I found my attention drawn from the powerful raptors nesting in the dead poplar to the tree itself. I saw the owl family less in the light of their own magnificence, and more in the subtle glow of their relationship with the dead tulip poplar and its tenants. Ultimately the tree became the magnetic presence that compelled my daily visits. I felt part of the deadwood community of life.

It was a magnificent tree and it literally rang with life.

The poplar was four feet across at its base. At thirty feet the trunk had forked evenly, but one of the forks had failed in a storm, leaving the wide platform on which the owls nested. The remaining fork slanted upward another forty feet, terminating abruptly below the surrounding canopy. The tree might have been a hundred years old when it died, about twenty years before my many visits. Very little bark remained, and its outer surface was pitted and pocked with the marks of insects and the excavations of predators who pursued them. The ground at the old poplar's base always was piled a foot deep with fresh wood chips. Above the nest platform the trunk was weathered gray and smooth, except for several dozen neat circular holes drilled by small and medium-sized woodpeckers.

Hiemal melted into prevernal. The parent owls didn't like my presence and they always knew when I was in my blind. Warily, they made occasional daytime feeding visits as the owlets grew. Between owl visits I watched the intensifying activity above and below their nest; eventually I reached a point at which I couldn't take my eyes off some other tenant's courtship, even to watch an owl antic.

The lengthening days quickened the flow of nuptial hormones

78

in the deciduous woodland's birds. The woodpeckers began to show territorial concern. And the dead poplar was clearly the focus of their attention. A noisy gaggle of flickers swooped to the highest snag and there sang and danced their *flick-a-flick-a-flick* routine by the hour. Sometimes up to six flickers would chase and flutter and posture about the patriarch poplar's broken skeleton. Occasionally a single flicker would preen and shriek his mating cadence from the dead tree's pinnacle.

Soon a pair of downy woodpeckers became interested in a two-foot span of trunk below the flickers. They tweeted and giggled, playing peekaboo from opposite sides of the snag. The female would fly to the snag and the male would follow in a fluttering display flight that suggested the wing movements of a bat.

A few feet lower, a pair of red-bellied woodpeckers took possession. A lone female tried for several days to insinuate herself into the family but, after repeated drubbings by the resident female (with the ambivalent assistance of the male), she yielded. I collected a pocketful of black and white mottled feathers before the contest ended.

There was no end to the Piciforms—woodpeckers—on the dead poplar. Eventually two more pairs of downies and a pair of hairies took leases at varying heights.

I hope somehow I can convey the sense of spectacle created by a half-dozen woodpecker families nesting in the same tree—above and below a pair of owls. The noise was awesome. There was hammering within and without. There was territorial drumming, a ritual staccato hammering on hollow wood to warn off rival males. There was fighting and teasing and mating. And there was uncommon carpentry. Chips and splinters rained from the vibrating trunk as old excavations were enlarged and refurbished and new holes were drilled. Periodically the young owls had to stand and shake the chips from their developing plumage.

Then one day there came from behind my blind a series of toots —loud and at quickening intervals. And up against the long-suffering poplar swooped a huge black and white bird, big as a crow. It was the pileated, largest remaining woodpecker in North America. I had heard the commanding voice on several previous visits to the blind, but now I could vividly associate it with the bird. The great woodsman cocked his red-crested head and the sun flashed in his eye. In two kicks, he vaulted six feet higher on the trunk and began to hammer. His head was a blurred red arc as he struck the brittle wood. His great silvery chisel stabbed and pried at the splinters and chunks fell audibly. In what seemed like a mere minute, a rectangular wedge six inches tall yawned in the side of the tree. The pileated cocked his head again and inquired verbally if anybody had anything to say about it. The owlets danced excitedly and peered curiously over the nest edge at the raucous proceedings; one of the parent birds in a nearby oak pretended not to notice. Then the great bird noisily launched himself and tooted away into the distant woods.

I went forward to inspect. Below the new excavation I picked up chips as big as matchbooks, splinters the size of pencils. Then I saw that the woodhen's (I think that's one of the nicest folk names for a wild thing) new wedge matched several others in the tree. The mass of the great poplar was formidable, but the years it could continue to withstand this assault were surely numbered.

The owls fledged toward the end of the prevernal. They had completed their nesting cycle a full season ahead of all other birds, perhaps for easier access to bird prey on the roosting perches before the leaves hid them. I noticed that the young were fed a higher proportion of bird prey than the adults ate.

As the owlets flapped clumsily and comically in the nearby trees, nesting began in earnest in their original, many-tiered apartment complex. Relatively few of the woodpeckers' cavities actively housed their builders. A pair of crested flycatchers took a vacant hole near the flickers' penthouse. Some bluebirds moved in below them, then chickadees, then Carolina wrens. A pair of white-breasted nuthatches scorned the woodpeckers' architecture and excavated their own nest hole. And, although neither I nor any of the nesters liked it much, two pairs of starlings raised successful clutches in the great brood tree.

Thirteen nests. Ten species. One dead tree. What more can I say?

Well, there are a few things more to be said in behalf of standing deadwood, although older forestry consultants won't necessarily agree. Some of the younger professionals are suggesting that we "plant a hardwood every tenth tree just for the raccoons and woodpeckers." But it wasn't so long ago that someone from somewhere in the departmental pancreas of the Great State of Virginia came through my family's farm and splashed orange stripes on every old den tree and misshapened hardwood on the place. It was his view that these trees should be removed to make way for more "productive" growth. The man may have been associated with the only bureaucracy in the world to emphasize productivity over stability. He listened politely to my story about the owl tree in College Park, but I doubt he was impressed. He just couldn't translate nuthatches into board feet.

One of the greatest tributes to the value of standing deadwood in a deciduous forest is paid by a forest which has none. The southern longleaf pine forests are virtually free of deadwood. Natural fires burn these forests regularly. The fires, to which the longleaf pines are resistant, arrest the succession process by burning the gums and turkey oaks. But at the same time the fires burn any standing deadwood as soon as the protective bark falls.

Alright, said the longleaf pine forest. We have no deadwood. Therefore we have no woodpeckers nor any other cavity-nesting birds. But these insects are eating us alive. We need some relief. Now!

Regrettably, this was a few million years before the U.S. Forest Service could apply any of its modern techniques to the plight of the pines, so they had to solve the problem themselves. In a flash of evolutionary genius, they found the red-cockaded woodpecker, the only bird which excavates into the living wood. This single species underpins the entire cavity-nesting avian and small-mammal community in the longleaf pine habitat. Every other woodpecker, plus flying squirrels, bees and many perching birds, can exist there only under the auspices of the red-cockaded woodpecker.

This is the kind of extra effort you need if you're a forest with no deadwood: you must create a new species. But the "cockade" represents an extreme of evolutionary specialization. There is no backup, no other creature to chew holes in the living wood if this bird fails. Among other things, Smokey the Bear's no-fire policy plus some indiscriminate clear cutting of the groves of nest pines nearly wiped out the red-cockaded woodpecker. It takes this bird five years to mine a single nest cavity in the resin-hard pine. But one night on an exposed limb, after the trees containing his roosting cavities have been cut, will put him in the gullet of a horned owl. So now the cockade is on the Rare and Endangered Species List. Only three thousand individuals now labor in the living pines to remind us how important it is to have deadwood in a deciduous forest.

This planet was endowed at birth with all the life-sustaining elements it will ever have. The carbon, nitrogen and phosphorus fixed in living tissue are scarce and must be recycled. So the owl tree must fall. It must rot and yield its energy and substance to another generation. For a few brief years after its death the poplar stands to shelter the creatures which groomed it while it lived. But even as it stands to give them haven, it falls.

There are forest fungi and bacteria which live by feasting on living wood. They are deemed parasites, just as they would be if they attacked living human tissue. But after a tree's death, often an agonizing process of gradual retreat before pathogenic attack rather than the sudden circulatory stoppage attending the death of an animal, a different set of fungi and bacteria take over —the saprophytes. These organisms invade the steel-strong woody structure. To make a very long and complex story absurdly short, the microbes soften the wood and make it palatable to higher organisms.

When the poplar died, the forks of its trunk held aloft hundreds of yards of leaf- and fruit-bearing twigs. The saprophytic micro-organisms attacked all parts of the tree uniformly; naturally the twigs softened first, next the smaller branches and so on. Then wind and perching birds and leaping squirrels snapped off those with smaller diameters, later breaking off successively larger pieces. The twig and small-branch material fell to the ground, to be further reduced by microbes and insects.

In the single nesting season that I watched, the woodpeckers and nuthatches must have shoveled out a hundred pounds of chips; to the ground this shredded wood fell, there to decompose. The topmost snag broke that spring, exactly at the center line of a woodpecker opening. The excavation had weakened the structure and wind had toppled the piece; it now lay near the tree's base.

The reduced mass and centralization of falling wood during this kind of natural reduction are important to the welfare of replacement trees. If the poplar had been felled alive by axe or storm, its careening tonnage would have crushed all the smaller trees below. Falling chip by chip, joint by woodpecker-weakened joint, its destructive force is nil, its lethal radius greatly shortened.

Even while the larger creatures tear at the softening boughs, they are helping to decompose the wood. Each broken twig, each chip pried from a nest cavity enlarges the surface area of wood available to fungal and bacterial attack.

But the great change of pace occurs when the trunk finally falls. By then the microbes have riddled the lignin of the structural members and broken down many of the more complex wood components into material digestible by insects. The liberation of wood-bound energy and nutrient then begins in earnest. All the carbon which the tree extracted from the carbon dioxide our grandparents breathed into the air; all the nitrogen which forest legumes like redbud and honey locust fixed in their root nodules and made available for the poplar's consumption; all the phosphorus and other mineral elements which the great tree stored during a century of growth; all these are released and metabolized by the forest floor wood decomposers as the trunk lies prone.

If the chewing and chiseling in the standing tree were notable, the silent workings within the fallen log are even more intense. A huge cast of characters enters the stage, playing coordinated and specialized roles in the decomposition process. These events liberate vast quantities of carbon dioxide directly into the atmosphere for the benefit of living trees. They also release heat; rotting logs often show through melting snow before their surroundings. And, of course, the process sustains the lives of the decomposers and their predators.

We can't see the carbon dioxide being released, and the heat is only indirectly visible. But the endless armies of wood decomposers are ours to observe. The precise function of each and the effects of their digestive chemistry upon the palatability of wood parts for subsequent diners is but sketchily comprehended. The

roles of certain fungi, certain bacteria and certain insects have been defined by intense, individual study but the whole process is still fairly vague to science. Also, to complicate their study, organisms vary with locality and wood type.

But this much can be said. Wood is not palatable to most insects (exceptions are the termites who host other organisms in their gut for the purpose). Fungi must usually predigest at least the more resistant components like lignin, tannin and resin. The fungi also soften wood's main constituent, cellulose, which is a lengthy polymer composed of sugars.

Fungi feast upon forest material by penetrating it with thread-like filaments called hyphae. These threads can be so minute

84

that an ounce of forest litter can contain two miles of them. Taken collectively as a fungal mycelium, the analog of a vascular plant's root system, they are the diaphanous filigrees of white or colored strands often seen lacing under a dead tree's bark. The mycelium unleashes chemicals upon the wood's components, extracting energy and substance to produce its fruiting bodies (mushrooms) and to fuel new growth.

The fruiting bodies of *some* wood-decomposing fungi are edible, but I won't take responsibility for differentiating edible from poisonous mushrooms. Much has been competently written on the subject and at best I would confirm only a half-dozen edible varieties. I will confess that I have eaten certain puffballs immediately after photographing them. They were exquisite—an icy morsel that left a nutty-sweet aftertaste in my mouth for hours.

When you see fungal fruiting bodies protruding from a standing tree, it is either dead or dying. Prostrate on the forest floor, a rotting tree trunk will likely host dozens of fungi in a year's cycle. If you pull away obviously rotten parts or if you can roll a rotting log ninety degrees, the array of fungi will astound you. There will also be slime molds, the plant or animal classification of which is still under debate because of their property of movement. But like the true fungi, the slime molds are highly associated with rotting wood. Their fruiting bodies rise like glistening fur or droplets of dye from the softening wood surface.

After the requisite preparation by fungi and bacteria, wood becomes palatable to certain insects. There must be scores; hundreds. One large beetle always comes quickly to mind because of its audible munching. This is the sawyer or long-horned beetle larva. A pine once died at the edge of my yard and all summer the sawyers chomped at its insides. The crunches came at one-second intervals, loud enough to be heard on my front porch seventy-five feet away. At some point, when I was trying to concentrate on something, the sawyers' munching began to grate on my nerves, so I went inside. I could still hear it.

Another time, an old oak blew down in a summer storm on my neighbor's farm and, in the fall, he let me cut up the great tree for firewood. When I split the big drums into manageable chunks I found another notable wood chewer. It was *Passalus,* a shiny

The wood-eating larva of the Passalus beetle munches audibly in deadwood.

black beetle an inch and a half long with powerful jaws and a short horn bending forward from its forehead. *Passalus* often succeeds the long-horned beetle in a dead tree, preferring to have its ration of wood undergo a bit more fungal softening than the sawyer. Colonies usually consist of just two adults and numerous white, wormy larvae. Exposed by my cutting, the adults lumbered from their galleries, salted with the chips of their tireless chewing. They made alarmed, whirring stridulations which, together with their slow, mechanical movements, made them seem like wind-up toys.

I was able to find some material on this insect which stated that the adults treat the rotting wood with a digestive secretion to make it edible by the larvae. This fact underscores the importance of the stridulations: they keep the *Passalus* family in communication within the galleries and, in effect, call the young to dinner.

Holding a *Passalus* in my fingers, I mused on the simplicity of this creature's life. No problems, I thought. All they have to do is eat the plentiful wood around them. The beetle swam mechanically in the air. Then I saw a tiny tick-like parasite, so flat that it moved comfortably about the beetle's underside in the paper-thin space between the thorax and the churning legs. Clearly this little red wafter had specialized on *Passalus,* probably tapping the great beetle's plumbing at leisure. So *Passalus* has its problems, too. Life is nowhere simple.

Passalus is prominent, but there are hordes of other wood-eating insects. Ants, stag beetles, bark beetles, borers, and many others chew the wood to tiny chips and pass the material through their digestive tracts. The excreta are then attacked by more fungi and bacteria; perhaps again by other invertebrates. Even the chips which don't pass directly through the animals have their surface areas vastly enlarged by the chewing and are thereby the more open to fungal attack.

The termite is a special wood eater. Some species don't need the predigestive attentions of fungi to make its wood helping palatable. It carries in its gut protozoa which can digest cellulose. No other animal is known to have that power in its digestive machinery, combined with mouth parts powerful enough to macerate fresh wood. Because they can tunnel into hard, newly dead wood, termites probably act as pioneers in the rot process by opening passageways into which airborne fungal spores can circulate.

Into this gustatory melee we must inject some noninsect invertebrates. Slugs and snails eat pathways through the little fields of slime mold and fungal fruiting bodies, fixing in their own tissue some of the carbon and nutrients which the fungi have liberated from the wood. They may also ingest some of the fungus-softened or insect-excreted wood material. Wood lice, millipedes and springtails feed on the decaying matter which, in the advanced stages we are discussing here, may bear little chemical or physical resemblance to the wood which first vibrated under the woodpecker's hammer.

Thus hundreds, maybe thousands, of creatures infect and spit their chemistry on and mouth and chew and digest and excrete the wood. Each step in the convoluted process breaks down the wood components into ever softer, ever simpler substances. Each wood-rot organism advances the process through its own assigned, if poorly comprehended, step, attacking a certain substance at a certain stage. The substances are constantly reduced toward such primal combinations as carbon dioxide, through which the vital elements—carbon, nitrogen, oxygen—flow out of death and back into life. In life and growth, these elements are synthesized into labyrinthine chemical associations—the endless organic polymers of specialized life functions. But in death and decay, they march with equal precision through a simplification process called rot, back to the basic foodstuffs stored in the soil and atmosphere.

*A millipede, differenti-
ated from the centipedes
by having two pairs of
legs per body segment
and by a vegetarian diet,
forages over a slime
mold on a rotting log.*

We have accounted for the wood components which the decomposers release as gases into the atmosphere. We have accounted for the solids which pass through the gastric treatment of successive legions of animals and fungi, to blend at last with the forest soil. But what of that ration of the tree's stored energy and nutrients which the decomposers fix in their own tissue?

Like any other group of primary heterotrophs, the wood decomposers have an associated company of secondary heterotrophs—their predators. Many are specialized to dwell in the newly hewn galleries and to feed upon the carpenters. Centipedes appear to be so oriented. They might be deemed the black-footed ferrets of decaying wood, preying on the insect prairie dogs. Prying apart chunks of decay, I have found a type of assassin bug lurking in the corridors, its tubular sucking mouth parts suitable for nothing save stabbing a victim and pumping out its body fluids. I have found a large beetle whose formidable pincer jaws resemble those of the aquatic hellgrammite, and I suspect that it too was a predator. In at least one instance, the fungi turn the tables on the deadwood insects and become diner rather than dinner. Insects breathe air bearing the spores of *Cordyceps,* a killer fungus. The spores germinate and riddle the insect with their mycelium. When the victim dies and *Cordiceps* has usurped its treasure of deadwood energy, the fungus sends up a colorful club-shaped fruiting body. With sinister beauty the little orange fingers protrude from the crevices of a log, marking the carcasses.

Like so many aspects of nature, you can observe and deduce the functions of deadwood organisms more readily than you can find literature to tell you about them. Precious little is available on decay organisms; still less on their predators. Scientists, to overcome the funding obstacles which dog them, tend to be very specific in their studies. They examine a certain organism in minutest detail. They focus less on a process and more on the function of an individual participant. And what they write is most intelligible to colleagues in related fields, but progressively less so to others as their interests diverge. To the layman, scientific papers are typically unintelligible.

But wood rot is only one of the many areas of inquiry in which the backyard naturalist must rely on his own academic and intui-

The grim but gaily-colored fruiting body of Cordiceps militaria, *a killer fungus, marks the grave of an insect deep in the galleries of this rotting log.*

tive foundation, however acquired. A balance must be struck by the citizen naturalist, between a search through the literature and pensive discovery in the field. Or woods. You can rapidly reach a point of diminishing returns in the library. But the horizons are ever wider in the woods.

For this is where you will observe things no one will ever tell you about. Things like the placement of a flicker's legs which gives it an adaptation—absent in all other woodpeckers—for feeding on the forest floor. And for picking and prying into prostrate rotting logs. You might, one day, top a little rise in the winter woods and spook a flicker from his ministrations to a log, the fresh chips and spongy fibers spinning in the wash of his wings. You know then that the flicker is an agent of wood decomposition; that is, an increaser of deadwood surface area, and a predator on wood-decay insects. And sometime you might see a bushel of fresh pryings strewn across a light snow around a log. The foot of a salamander, mysteriously uneaten, tells you that a raccoon somehow smelled the hibernating amphibian within and ripped away the rotting wood. The raccoon, too, is an unwitting wood-decay agent; and the salamander a predator on wood-decay insects.

And so it goes. No more than I can indifferently pass by a thistle in bloom can I pass a hulk of rotting wood without rolling it over (if I can) to see who's there. A worm snake pursuing the earthworms who do the final mixing of deadwood and soil? A narrow-mouthed toad squeezing its seemingly boneless body into a crevice you would think only a liquid could penetrate? The ants look like they're giving the toad a bad time now that I have exposed and terrified it. Insects' revenge?

Probing an old deadwood hulk, a narrow-mouthed toad makes the mistake of intruding upon an ant colony.

6 / *Winter Birds*

THE HIBERNAL SUN tracks low across the southern horizon, slanting weakly through the naked trees. Under this niggardly ration of sunshine, colors fade and the pace of life slows. Each plant and creature in the temperate latitudes deals with this shortage in its own way. Methods vary, but a common theme unites them all in parsimony—*make yourself scarce.*

The adult insects die, at least the visible ones whose nature exposes them to outdoor rigors. The young overwinter as eggs, larvae and pupae. Some spiders overwinter as adults, like the little salticids who wrap themselves for warmth and camouflage in a silken envelope that pokes and bulges unconvincingly at the least disturbance. But many endure the cold as eggs in an insulated bundle tucked into a protective crevice. Turtles and lizards bury themselves in decomposing forest litter and recapture the slow seepage of rot-liberated solar energy, breathing weakly. Or they burrow into the muck of a stream or lake bed and give up breathing altogether. Like masses of hibernating entrails, snakes slither together in clusters to conserve heat during their winter sleep. Plants die back to the soil or shed their exposed soft tissue, flush out their freezable fluids and settle in behind protective bark and bud scales. Or else die completely and overwinter as seeds (which sometimes depend on being freeze-treated before the germination sequence can be activated). Mammals hibernate, some sleeping deeply and continuously, others arising to move stiffly in brief foraging forays, still others eating sparingly of the

92

plant matter they cached for the lean season. The few that hunt do so with careful investment of energy designed for the maximum and quickest return. The fungi lie laced through the soil and deadwood, not daring to proffer a fruiting body to the cold world outside.

The birds that eat flying insects, like the insects, vanish. They must go to the tropics or, even further, to the southern temperate zones where summer is raging. Gone are the swifts, the swallows, the martins, the cuckoos, the nighthawks, the whippoorwills, the flycatchers, the indigo buntings, the blue grosbeaks. Gone is the score of wood warblers who groomed the great oaks in the summer sun, gleaming like jewels in the green crowns. Gone are the thrushes and robins and vireos who nabbed caterpillars, stopping them in midmunch on the foliage. Gone is the gnatcatcher, picking his nits somewhere to the south, and the hummingbird gone from the stream.

Yet we are not alone. We have the winter birds.

Subtract from the surging density of summer birdlife all those who catch flying and crawling insects. Take away also those seed-eaters, like the bobolink and the blue grosbeak, whose heritage includes intercontinental travels for good and valid reasons, if known only to them. But add the precious few eaters of seeds and berries who arrive from the far north. You now have the wintering birds.

But not the *winter* birds.

Here again we wrestle with the metaphysical, the interpretive in nature. For there are some birds who winter *near* us but not *with* us. They spurn our offerings. They prefer a completely natural lifestyle free of any involvement with the strange biped who sometimes comes in peace, sometimes to destroy, but always to leave his mark on the homelands of wild things. In short there are some birds who will have no truck with man.

The winter wren, for example, in spite of its name, is not a "winter bird" to me because it is a secretive creature who flits surreptitiously among the exposed tree roots along the streambanks. I have never heard of one patronizing a backyard feeding station. You may happen upon a winter wren deep in the woods, usually near water, but like as not it will flit and jibber briefly

93

*The brown creeper is an
example of a "non-
winter" bird. It lives
near us (but not with us)
in winter, spurning all
association with humans,
disappearing against the
tree bark in its superb
camouflage.*

before you, then somehow disappear, like a mouse under a stump.

Likewise the brown creeper comes from the north to spend the winter as a ghostly shading in the tree bark. The creeper doesn't totally reject man like the winter wren: it simply doesn't believe man exists. It is most often seen in the deep woods skittering ever upward on the tree trunks in short fits and starts, disappearing totally when at rest. When it reaches thirty-odd feet of height on an oak trunk, it flies down to the base of the next tree. If the next tree happens to be in your yard, the creeper couldn't care less. But don't count on it ever coming back.

We catch fleeting glimpses of crossbills and siskins in little feeding cliques, foraging for whatever it is they fancy, at a height of fifty feet in the red oak's bark. Golden-crowned kinglets maneuver over the high twigs in the pines and gums, very much involved with one another, but uninterested in man or his leavings.

We do not dispute these birds' taste in rejecting us. The history of man's attitude toward the birds has not always been dominated by sympathetic understanding, so we really can't complain. We simply recognize that, for whatever reasons, there are some wintering birds we rarely see unless we go forth all bundled and binoculared for that purpose and no other. No, these birds are not a force in our lives in winter. They are not winter birds.

But, oh, the waves of evening grosbeaks that fill our windowsills with black and white and gold. Big, proud, forward birds with voices clear as chimes. Could another creature be more a part of my life than the sentinel male who commanded the feeding flock from atop the spruce outside my breakfast window? His colors against the fierce blue of the morning after last year's first snowstorm welcomed me to winter. And, ah, the cardinal at the feeder that flashes his crest in dominance, the purple finches that squabble at his side, the towhee that scratches like a chicken at what they toss to the ground. These are the birds with whom we conspire to see past February's chill. The juncos gleaning peacefully with the white-throated sparrows beneath the feeder and the nuthatch laughing at us as it runs upside down along the bottom of a limb. Winter birds all.

And why? Well, vague as the notion seemed to me at first, I eventually became satisfied that there are certain birds who come

94

into our awareness in winter merely by their willingness to accept humans as part of their world. Those, to me, are the winter birds. So the formula becomes:

$$(\text{Summer birds} - \text{emigrants} + \text{immigrants}) - \text{the reclusive types} = \text{Winter birds}$$

As in the formula for plant photosynthesis, sunlight is the catalyst that makes it go. Sunlight, packaged as seeds, as fruits and insects, feeds the winter birds. Gulping the tablets of stored solar energy, the winter birds move with reckless alacrity against their dormant and colorless background, defying the energy shortage that has grayed-out the rest of nature. The few cold-tolerant insects and the seeds and persistent fruits of a few key plants yield the power; and the winter birds convert it to the tireless flashes of colorful movement that brighten our shrubbery and spirits when they need it most.

A varied set of rhythms brings the winter birds together with us, or into our awareness if they were already present. Some, like the chickadees and titmice, are with us all year, but only in winter do they urge themselves upon us. In warmer months they are shy retiring forest elves who nest and forage on the fringe of our awareness. In winter they become the bold and tiny scolds who shower us with imprecations for our alleged improvidence the instant we step outside. Cardinals and towhees likewise share with us the fortunes of all seasons, but ignore us when insects are plentiful; they blend easily into the wealth of summer's color. The homebody mockingbird grows cantankerous in winter, peevishly driving seed-eating birds away from the food it cannot swallow until we relent and share our raisins. The goldfinch, a flying flower in his bright summer garb, spurns then our shrubbery for thistles in the open pasture. But in cold months he visits the seed feeder in a drab disguise, as if to deny that winter could reduce the carefree "wild canary" to alms-taking.

Others attend us only as wintering migrants. Their arrivals and departures mark the limits of winter for us; their visits spice the icy interim. The purple finch comes by Christmas—by Thanksgiving, if severe weather rages early over the North. The raspberry males perch in dignity while their sparrow-brown ladies haggle

96

over the fare. Evening grosbeaks are irregular migrants who favor us with their colors only in selected winters. Cedar waxwings winter in the southern half of the country, feeding in groups of a score or two on persisting tree fruits like black gum and holly and on the berries of shrubs and herbs. They rarely come to seed feeders, but a holly or a pyracantha bush by your house will gain you the special treat of a feeding flock of waxwings once or twice a winter.

There are several vertebrate groups whose primary interest is seeds. Certain rodents, notably mice and squirrels, concentrate on seeds. They even maintain inventories stored for later use. Deer eat quantities of acorns, the seeds of oaks. And man is no mean fancier of seeds. Cereal grains, the seeds of grasses, enable his

A male evening grosbeak stands guard in a spruce top over his feeding flock.

97

societies to live in the manner to which they have become accustomed.

Among North American perching birds there is a family, the *Fringillidae*, which specializes in seeds; any member of the family is easily identified as such by the heavy conical bill specifically adapted to cracking them. The grosbeaks, cardinals, towhees, finches, sparrows, buntings and juncos are fringillids. The mandibles of the evening grosbeak, for example, are said to be capable of cracking a cherry pit. Mine can't.

The seeds of the grasses and legumes which this family favors are readily available, protruding from the snow on stout stems in many regions; so their food supply permits fringillids to winter fairly far north. Some move to wintering ranges moderate distances to the south of their breeding latitudes. Others, like the cardinal, winter where they nest. A few very northerly types like the redpolls and the crossbills irregularly visit as far south as the Great Lakes in winter.

But a great many fringillids winter in the more temperate regions. The size of the family and the strapping populations of the individual species, combined with a robust cold tolerance, make *Fringillidae* the premier winter bird family across the continent. Basically, they are the ones who camp at our seed feeders and shell huge piles of expensive sunflower seed.

There are other winter birds who relish seeds. Their eating habits, however, differ from those of fringillids. Chickadees, titmice, woodpeckers, nuthatches and bluejays hold the seeds with their feet or wedge them into a bark crevice, then hammer them open. The fringillids shell them in their mouths and eject the hulls as deftly as a human spitting grape seeds (which, by the way, are legitimate fringillid fare). The non-fringillid seed-eaters typically take a range of food and may even specialize in something other than seeds, while still retaining the versatility to enjoy them occasionally.

The eaters of fruit are functionally akin to the seed-eaters because fruit contains seeds. In fact, some seeds are surrounded by fruits for the specific purpose of getting the seeds into a bird's digestive tract. Poke seeds, for example, do not germinate until scarified by a bird's digestive chemistry. The seed coat is so resistant that it must be weakened by the birds, but it will not dissolve enough to liberate the contents inside the birds. The fruit, however, must be of immense food value to them, for many birds seem to eat little else while the purple berries hang in grapelike bunches. The purple droppings containing undigested seeds stain the countryside.

Even the fruit-covered seeds which can germinate without passing through a bird often gain a higher percentage of germination by doing so. They also gain transport to new and better places. So we can comfortably conclude that the plants wrapped their seeds in a tasty fruit to attract birds (or other animals) no less than they surrounded their sexual parts with colorful flowers filled with sweet nectar to attract pollen-bearing insects. It works out well all around because birds have short and, some would say, inefficient digestive tracts. Unlike an ungulate, a bird cannot afford to haul around a third of its body weight as slowly digesting food. Avian digestive tracts seem just long enough to utilize the fruits and to give the seeds an assist in germinating.

Blueberries and blackberries are quickly eaten as they ripen in mid- and late summer. Poke and wild grapes are moderately durable; they appear to serve the birds through the fall migration. But the berries of a few wild shrubs and trees persist until April unless eaten. Holly and red cedar are examples. Black gum berries would probably also persist until April if they weren't gobbled away in a relentless orgy. The woodland shrubs, Viburnum and strawberry bush, offer berries until Christmas. And the little black beads on honeysuckle are available throughout the cold months. When we include the berries of cultivated shrubs like privet, nandina and pyracantha, there are many fruits available to those winter birds who want them. Naturally, there are many takers.

The mockingbird (once strictly a southerner but now in the process of exporting his rebelliousness northward) and the related brown thrasher are berry fanciers *extraordinaire*. The robins and bluebirds on their wintering grounds and our only wintering thrush, the hermit, all concentrate on persistent fruits in winter. The Carolina wren helps himself. And the cedar waxwings, with oriental politeness, shuttle from the bare elm in my yard to the berry-laden cedars and hollies. They never squabble among themselves; they never respond to the mockingbird's attack except to *whee-whee* a demure apology and yield the feeding grounds. But when unmolested, they sit for long sessions casually gulping berries from around their heads or even passing them generously from mouth to mouth. As the charming ritual goes on, you find that the waxwings are the "berry children" among winter birds. Through the season's harshness they caress and feed and sing to one another by the hour. If the eaters of seeds and the eaters of porkchops have something to squabble over, that is of no concern to the waxwings.

The seed-eaters are basically alike—with different sizes, songs and colors, but essentially the same shapes and equipment. The fruit-eaters are more varied. Several families are involved, and the shapes and lifestyles aim at different opportunities. A third dietary group confronts us with even greater diversity—the insect-eaters.

Winter's insects are few and elusive. Yet they support a small but vibrant and visible staff of bird predators from vastly different families. The endless swarms of summer's flying insects draw the undivided attention of countless birds specializing in every conceivable capture technique. But where I live a single flycatcher, the eastern phoebe, hawks the winter insects. The phoebe launches deadly strikes from a prominent bare twig and returns to precisely the same spot to gulp down its victim. Pleased, she wipes her bill on the twig, flips her tail downward and snaps her one-note chirp. I have watched my resident phoebe extensively but have never been able to see the insect prey in its flight; they seem to be visible only to the phoebe. Toward winter's end, she begins roosting under my porch eaves and in the early spring raises her brood there. I could never be persuaded that the phoebe is not a winter bird.

The ruby-crowned kinglet is the tiniest winter bird in the east. It is scarcely larger than a female hummingbird, and it can hover before a spinning flight of winter midges like a hummingbird at a flower. The bird is colored like an olive and shaped like a teardrop. A white ring encircling the eye is its most outstanding marking; wing bars are visible at rest. But the bird never is at rest.

The kinglet is a blur of violent industry too quick for the eye to follow as it duplicates the erratic courses of its prey—the minute flying insects of winter. The ruby is visible on the heads of the males only when they want it to be; otherwise, it is completely retracted.

The bluebirds and their allies (hermit thrushes and robins) enjoy a mixed fruit and insect diet in winter. Two warblers, the pine and the myrtle, are common in winter where I live but not too much further north. The pine warbler forages in the crowns of trees, especially pine, and the myrtle hunts the middle story and shrub strata. Southward, several additional wood warblers comb the winter vegetation for small insects. The bluebirds and warblers, along with the Carolina wren, also relish a mixture of peanut butter, bacon fat and cornmeal, when the mockingbird doesn't divebomb them away from the table. Seeing them gulp down great mouthfuls of such human fare at my window sill obligates me to include them among the winter birds. Robins rarely eat a human offering, but they love the winter worms and grubs in our yards. And they're real hygiene enthusiasts—break the ice in your bird bath and, often as not, the robins will make you shiver at the sight of their icy ablutions.

Now we get to the real insect gourmets: woodpeckers and nuthatches. Their air-hammer approach to food procurement resounds through all seasons, diminished not a whit by the cold. Because no shelf in the forest pantry is too high or hard for them, most woodpeckers have no need to migrate. If the cold drives the beetle larvae deeper into the deadwood, the woodpeckers dig deeper. Their hammering guides us through the bare gray woods and, returning at eventide, a downy may swoop over us, to retire squeaking and jibbering into his roosting cavity. The red-headed woodpecker comes south a bit but still claims most of the eastern United States as his wintering grounds. The yellow-bellied sapsucker, of course, must move to latitudes where the sap seeps year-round from the wounded cambium. He drills his wells in neat horizontal rows in oak and maple and sweet gum and fruit wood, returning later to lap out the sweetness. And right behind the sapsucker, in blatant accessory to his vandalism, come the cardinal, the Carolina wren, and just about every other winter bird that enjoys the weeping confections. No less than human consumers whose demand stimulates production and pollution, the winter birds pilfer the sapsucker's syrups, forcing him to inflict his minor phlebotomies on more and more trees.

The nuthatches appear to be woodpeckers from the neck up, mice from the neck down. They move about over every surface of a tree, assuming every angle and contortion as if they alone were exempted from the force of gravity. They can run headfirst down a tree trunk and catch a falling morsel of suet. They are known to drill their own nesting cavities and to use abandoned woodpecker holes. The largest nuthatch, the white-breasted, is smaller than the smallest woodpecker, the downy. Therefore, heavy construction is more associated with woodpeckers than with nuthatches, who concentrate on prying insect fugitives from bark crevices. It is the nuthatches' thoroughness that intrigues us. They use their gymnastics to scrutinize every niche, no matter how inaccessible. And even in the dead of winter you can sometimes see them extracting a fat grub and squeaking excitedly.

The nuthatches and some woodpeckers will accept sunflower seeds. They *all* like suet, the chunks of animal fat given to us by our friendly village butcher or sold for a small charge by our almost-as-friendly supermarket operator. The woodworkers and such other birds as chickadees and titmice utilize this stored power to sustain their high metabolic rate and to make it through weather which might otherwise be foul enough to claim them. It's easy to notice that the birds consume suet at a rate directly related to the harshness of the weather. The fat is devoured during a snowstorm, ignored on an unseasonably warm sunny day. Suet has the capacity to draw a major congregation to your feeding station from deep within the naked woodlots. Without this fatty attraction, some birds can find no basis for any relationship with man, and we might not have known them as winter birds.

It's all quite arbitrary and capricious, this business of recognizing some as winter birds while excluding others. But a burgeoning wild-bird feeding industry appears to be based on this interpretation. Besides, it is the birds who are selective, not the people.

Today is February 9, 1975. Dawn broke an hour ago, overcast. I sit before my breakfast room window, certain of my thoughts with the little sharp-shinned hawk which yesterday flushed from the woods behind the garden a cresting wave of robins toward me. My inner feet march lightly to the different drummer that keeps me comfortably out of step with the world of shopping centers, with bins of fruits and vegetables individually sealed in plastic as if the pesticides might otherwise escape. But I'm still uncomfortably aware that it's the only world I've got. I squirm. Better, I think, to concentrate on the seed feeder ten feet on the other side of my window; or on the slab of suet strapped to the tree. Better to rejoice in the real world that's left around me. The plastic is a figment. Soon it will be gone. Like the marvelous lead plumbing that poisoned Rome, it will one day set scientists to jabbing at one another with pipe stems and clucking at the naive technologies of the ancients.

Last evening a late "feed" nearly emptied the seed feeder. I open the door. The birds scatter. I fill the bin with sunflower seed, re-enter and discard the empty plastic bag.

A pane of glass six feet square separates me from the feeder. A screen separates the birds from the glass. Without the screen the birds mistake the glass for a clear passage and the carnage is horrible. A half-hour ago, in the day's first light, I addressed a drum of oak with wedge and sledge hammer, for me a ritual outpouring of any frustrations my dreams did not ventilate. The quartered oak crackles now in the fireplace behind me and as in Aldo Leopold's early morning vigils, in *A Sand County Almanac,* the coffee pot whets my senses. I am ready to record the goings-on at the feeding stations.

A chickadee tumbles from the cover of a nearby big cedar and hits the feeder, scolding, before I am back in the house. Like the spring ephemeral wildflowers, he has grabbed his ration and run before the big boys got into the act. He holds the sunflower seed to a limb with his feet and manfully hammers it open. The slightly larger tufted titmouse does not have to be quite so bold; she allows a few moments for the dust of my disturbance to settle, then, in a quick pass, grabs a single seed and duplicates the chickadee's hammering.

103

Now come the purple finches, a group of half a dozen, leapfrogging past one another through the branches. Their advance seems to be a game: "Let the other fellow go first and expose himself to danger, but I can't stand it if he gets to the feeder first so I'll pass him." A female lands on the feeder. Then another. A squabble ensues. The feeder has two seed-dispensing sides, mind you, but the female finches go to the same side and fight over it. One prevails and the loser retires to a limb. Then returns for further squabble. So far neither has eaten a seed. The chickadee steals one while the fracas rages. Finally, the two females claim opposite corners and settle in, shelling seed after seed without moving. The males, having disdainfully witnessed the warfare, begin to alternate at the opposite shelf, feeding in relative peace. The chickadees and titmice visit, as prudence permits, each pass made with the timing and trepidation of a runner stealing a base.

Now a goldfinch arrives, transformed from the brilliant garb in which it plucked the down from last aestival's thistle. The goldfinch, scarcely more than half the purple finch's size, stands up to the female purple finch's attack—and wins! (Although I suspect the purple finch may have eaten about all she wanted anyway.) The goldfinch, too, is a stationary feeder, firmly occupying a spot at the ledge and showering the ground with sunflower shells.

And millet, for which none of the birds yet mentioned cares very much. The frosted ground is by now crisscrossed by a hopping blur of juncos and white-throated sparrows. Neither bird can bring itself to sit at the feeder. Nor can the towhee who just arrived to scatter the smaller fringillids. They scratch and hop and pick over every square inch again and again, salvaging the spilled grain. As they dance, I begin to note who's who in the pecking order. The juncos come in a variety of sizes and colors. The immature birds are brown-backed, the females grayer, and the mature males almost black above the stark countershading of their white bellies. White is visible in the outer tail feathers of all the juncos when they fly, but on the ground the white is demurely covered. Except by a big male who scatters the others, dashing through the flock flashing his white "V" and claiming the best pickings. He is clearly alpha junco.

Toward the edge of the circle of ground feeders, I notice a large, brownish bird with rusty flecks on its breast. My thrasher, I mark with satisfaction, having been concerned at his absence for the past few days. But no! It has a thrasher's body but the beak of a fringillid. A fox sparrow! I should have known from the bird's agreeable demeanor that it wasn't my brown thrasher, whose first gesture usually is to charge and disperse all other gleaners. The fox sparrow, the first I've seen this year, hunkers quietly and pops the paper-thin hulls off the millet. The fox-red tail and coverts mark him as the largest sparrow in the east.

Back at the feeder, the scene has changed from brown and purple to black and gold. The evening grosbeaks are mustering. They make no violent gestures on arrival, to other birds or to one another. Yet they quickly become sole occupants by virtue of their size. They settle in and shell sunflower seeds. Piles of them. The grosbeaks alternate at the feeder; the smaller birds cluster hungrily in the nearby branches. Twenty minutes pass. The grosbeaks have measurably lowered the level of seed in the bin.

The colors shift abruptly once more, this time to blue. The bluejay is one of the few birds formidable enough to displace the grosbeaks. But, again, the grosbeaks are full and the bluejay brazen with hunger. The grosbeaks' irritated chimes fade; the bluejay briefly shrieks its triumph, then falls to feeding. It grabs a seed, tilts its head back and swallows, again and again. I used to think bluejays were endowed with special plumbing capable of digesting the sunflower seed coats. But avian insides are designed to save weight; cast iron stomachs are too heavy. So the intestines are short, and the crop, in many birds, separates the unusables for immediate regurgitation. I keep an eye on the bluejay. It flies to the edge of the woods, coughs up a seed, holds it against the limb with a foot and shatters the protective seed coat with a single blow.

The feeder is like the center of a kaleidoscope with new colors converging on it from all sides and old colors simultaneously outbound. Blue is out, red is in. The cardinal has always seemed to me a misplaced bird of the tropics. It is by far the most colorful of the winter birds and, with the possible exception of the painted bunting, is perhaps the brightest bird on the continent.

105

Trapping air in their contour feathers, a cardinal and his lady take on the rosy pinks that a snowstorm somehow reflects in their plumage.

Two males now spar at the feeder. A third arrives and the first two flee as if the newcomer were a hawk. Alpha cardinal erects his crest and postures briefly on the ledge, then digs in. He cracks a seed, then scratches several to the ground for his retinue of ladies and for the lesser males he just evicted.

106

And so it goes. I have passed an hour watching the badinage of colors between the major winter birds at or under the feeder. Occasionally a less frequent visitor takes a few seeds—a chipping sparrow, a downy woodpecker, a redwing, a field sparrow, a cowbird. A pair of mourning doves whiffles to the ground, beads of iridescence gleaming down the sides of the male's neck. A white-breasted nuthatch arcs in, emitting its endless snickers. It grabs a seed and arcs out again to wedge the seed in a bark crevice and hack it open. The titmice and chickadees never miss an opportunity. And every so often the feeder dances under the impact of a red-bellied woodpecker who, like the bluejay, scatters the smaller diners and hauls off a cheekful of seeds to be opened at leisure.

At lunchtime, I smear another big spoonful of the peanut butter-bacon fat-cornmeal goo on the maple's bark. A kinglet appears, hangs sideways, then upside down, and finally picks off several mouthfuls while hovering. He retires to a nearby shrub and wipes his beak on a twig. Suddenly his crest becomes visible. He flits nervously through the shrub as if pursuing midges, then takes off and crosses fifty yards of open lawn to attack another kinglet in another shrub. From this distance I cannot see the bodies of the tiny birds, but their erected crests look like two red Christmas lights gyrating in the shrub's interior. One flees, the other's crest subsides, and both meld into the wind-tossed detritus of winter vegetation.

A bluebird hovers briefly, touching the air gently with her wingtips. She clings to the bark and gobbles. A myrtle warbler appears, not hostile but businesslike in spite of the lemon-gold foppery about his rump and shoulders. Soon both are back in the branches, wiping the white flecks from their bill bristles.

I seldom see just one or two birds at the feeders. They all arrive together for a "feed" and depart together when either finished or frightened. They return more quickly if the feeder is handy to some protective shrubbery into which they can retire every few minutes to rest. Or to escape the hawks that lurk in the sky and in their minds.

Ah, you say, hawks are a thing of the past. I live in town where there are no hawks to molest any birds.

Well, more than one urban bird-lover has been treated to the spectacle of a sharp-shinned hawk blitzing through the yard to snag a grosbeak off the feeder and pluck it on the spot. The winter birds move into the towns and cities because that's where the people are. And people mean sunflower seed and pyracantha. The little sharp-shin, the male hardly bigger than a robin, finds it can winter unobtrusively in the parks and gardens and help himself to the urban winter birds. It is possible, just possible, to witness this ancient and essential drama even in the heart of a big city. The sharp-shin is part of the ordained North American life scheme. He is entitled to his prey, rural or downtown.

Not so the domestic housecat, a creation of man's genetic tampering. *Felis catus* probably never existed anywhere in the wild and certainly is not a natural or legitimate predator in North America. I never stopped to think of it this way until a neighbor of mine once asked me into his yard, pointing to a cat in a cage-type trap and asking if it were my cat. It was, and what, I demanded, was it doing in that trap?

"That's what I want to know," he said. "If you're going to keep a cat, keep it—the hell away from my birds. Like in your house."

The neighbor explained, and I ultimately came to agree, that the houescat's hunting instinct makes it a formidable threat to birds and small mammals. The cat is new on the scene and the prey is not genetically endowed with defenses against it. The two did not "grow up" together over zoologic time. And, most diabolically, cats fed at home and turned loose on the neighborhood to "play," use the energy subsidy we give them to harass the legitimate wildlife. It's not the cats' fault. It's ours.

Evening nears. I return to my bird-viewing chair. The feeders and the ground are aswarm with fringillids. Suddenly they flush, except for a few juncos who freeze to the ground. A huge spear-shaped bird arcs in, wings folded, then swoops upward and fastens to the maple's trunk. Warily, but loudly, the red-bellied woodpecker backs down the trunk toward the suet. He will feed lustily with the setting sun before retiring to his roosting cavity. But his approach to the suet is accompanied by a litany of hoots and a ritual of cautious assents and dissents, of disappearances to peerings from the "safe" side of the tree. He is like a man

108

building courage to dash into a flaming house to save a treasure. Then, with contrasting cool, the nuthatch hitches headlong down the maple trunk, sounding its mischievous yawks and giggles to pre-empt the larger bird at the suet cake.

The shadows lengthen, then fade. Bird after bird retires. The feeding conversation thins. Now I hear only the metallic clicks of the juncos—something like ice cracking on a pond—and the faint, plaintive inquiries of the white-throated sparrows. How totally, I muse, these two birds mean winter to me. If I heard their voices in a summer evening I would be subconsciously confused and anxious long before I knew why. The junco is called "snow-bird," for its migrations closely follow the edge of winter and the ground on which it feeds is often white with snow. The white-throat is a close relative, but lingers awhile in spring after the junco decamps. Both birds now feed on, their shapes visible only when they move, their colors faded into the day's afterglow.

Then they, too, are gone. I open the door and stand on the porch to feel the bite of the winter dusk. As if on signal, the white-throats break into song, shattering the evening's quiet with their only outburst of the day. The fifteen minutes that precede hibernal darkness are given over entirely to the surging chorus of the white-throats. Their explosive, high-pitched *BEEET* sounds at one-second intervals from the roosting perches in every shrub and cedar. I could not say how many winter evenings the rising white-throat crescendo has bid me hurry to gather kindling for the fire.

7 / The Courtship of the Grasses

IF YOU ASKED the chairman of the Federal Reserve Board what is the basis of the American economy he would likely tell you it is the dollar. Any politician worthy of the term "evasive" would give you a litany of basic truths involving free enterprise and profits and whatever else he thinks you might be pleased to hear. And since one-seventh of the American work force depends on the automotive industry, any of that group would hasten to affirm that the automobile is the foundation of our economy. Its welfare cannot sag; its numbers must proliferate. Today, of course, the avant-garde thinking is that *energy* sustains our economy. Oil in particular. And regrettably, oil is controlled by villainous desert nomads into whose swarthy hands an unkind fate has delivered unthinkable power to affect our standard of living.

But another school of thought contends that the foundation of our livelihood is not oil. Nor is it money, nor even the automobile. It is grass.

Sophistry, you say. Nay, a nature freak's avoidance of modern commercial realities. Grass, indeed! Why not dandelions or rutabagas or salt or ice cream or emeralds?

Observe.

By grass(es), I refer to that family of herbaceous plants, the *Poaceae*, an immense family of six hundred genera worldwide. Ten thousand years ago, at most, man learned to cultivate certain grasses—wheat, barley and corn—the better to gather and grind their nutritious seeds. It was the greatest single achievement in hominid history. Without the cultivation of cereal and forage grasses, there would have been no domesticated livestock, no wheel, no lunar landing. There would have been no social man.

More than half the world's people today eat rice and little else. Rice is a grass. If a single grass species were to be selected as most important, it must surely be *Oryza sativa*: Rice. The other part of humanity feeds on corn or barley or wheat or rye or oats, or on any of a score of other cereal grasses. Sometimes, for the very affluent, these grains are first run through a domesticated ungulate that fixes perhaps ten percent of the grasses' food value in its flesh—a profligate use of the grain. But usually even western man takes his grass straight, harvesting and drying the seeds, then grinding and cooking them. The recipes are as varied as they are sustaining.

Bamboo, too, is a grass, the structural lumber of the orient. All the cereal grains are grasses. Sorghum and sugarcane and most of the major forage crops are grasses. Name an economically important herbaceous plant and it will likely be a grass. A few which are commonly thought to be grasses, however, are not. Sedges and rushes are called grasslike plants but are not true grasses. Grasses have round stems, thin bladelike leaves. Sedges usually have triangular stems; most rushes have round leaves. Alfalfa, clover and lespedeza are legumes (the bean family), not grasses, although they are typical lawn plants. Marijuana is not a grass.

All things considered, I think we live in (or on) a grass economy. Large, opulent, artistic, highly successful human societies have existed without oil, automobiles or money. None ever made it without grass. It is the same today.

So where does that leave us?

About halfway along, I'd say. We've gone about as far as we can go with the grasses economically. We can now bend to the aesthetic harvest. The grasses have propelled our numbers from a few million Cro-Magnon hunter-gathers to nearly four billion coolies and suburbanites. They have pushed our spacecraft deep into the solar system and our aspirations far beyond. Oh, we might, if we want to take the risks, squeeze another doubling of our population from the Poaceae. Temporarily. But, I submit,

111

the horizon of economic benefit derivable from the grasses is clearly in sight. Their beauty, however, is largely untapped. And it rivals their wealth. No form of beauty could be more accessible than the flowers of the grasses; yet none is more frequently over-looked. Again, we must scale down our perceptions to see another life scheme.

Suppose you were a little red linyphiid spider toiling and spin-ning in some human's lawn. Your life lurches with the rhythms of the huge helicopter that comes by once a fortnight in the summer and dissolves your world in a maelstrom of noise and whirling blades. After it passes, the grass forest you live in is only half as tall as before, and your web is obliterated. This sort of thing hap-pens from time to time and, though nothing in your genes tells you precisely how to deal with it, you retire to your hiding place down under and wait for the wee hours. At which time a message comes telling you to build another web, to have it in place by sunrise.

The first light catches in the crystal globes hanging in your new web. Still larger globes gleam in the ragged grass tops. For a few minutes the sunlight dances in a thousand lenses. Soon the lenses quietly evaporate. You catch two or three gnats rising from the matted litter, on their way to zing in the ears of creatures too large to contemplate. You fang them lovingly, inject the digestive fluids and deftly swaddle each kill in silk. By the time the morning flight is over, you note that they have ceased to struggle, signify-ing that their insides have liquified. You refang to form a stable bridge over which the juices can flow and suck your victims dry. Delicious! You clean the excess off the sensory hairs on your legs and pedipalps and burp a tiny froth of bubbles. Replete, you retire beneath a blade and listen to the grass grow.

And grow it does. Noisily. Rapidly. Each morning in the wee hours you eat yesterday's web and spin another, a story higher as the stems lengthen. And one morning the sunlight gleams about you in crystal globes dangling along a spike of the grass' flowers. Embedded in each glassy sphere are purple fronds (to a human your size they would suggest ostrich plumes) and ruddy parentheses back to back on long white filaments. Basking in the beauty of your private, but living, Steuben collection, you note

112

with sadness that the business and perspective of some creatures deny them these delights.

Grasses, too, are flowering plants, though we fail to see them as such. Is it simply a question of size? Perhaps not. Oak and maple and elm trees are flowering plants no less than grasses and rose bushes. The red maple, champion shade tree of the east, fairly glows red with inflorescence under the young prevernal sun. The wild onion bristling from our lawns in winter is a flowering plant. In short, every plant that grows from a seed, excepting the conifers and a few very primitive plants like the cycads and the ginkgo, must first have a flower to unite the male and female germ cells. A seed is only a fertilized plant

A tiny red linyphiid spider hangs upside-down in her dew-jeweled web in the grass.

*Orchard grass, a common
lawn grass, in full flower.*

egg surrounded by enough food to give the young plant a start in life.

Whether or not we perceive a plant as a flower producer depends, I think, on the vehicle the plant uses to convey the pollen from the anther to the stigma. If birds or bees are involved, the plant displays colorful bracts and petals and exudes sweet scents to attract them. Flowers, to be sure. But if wind is the pollinator, ostentation has no function. And like the oak and onion, grasses are wind pollinated. Therefore what is needed is *lots* of flowers with (relatively) huge netlike stigmas sifting the breeze for pollen. And pollen must be produced in great quantities.

These, in essence, are the mechanics of wind-pollinated sex. It is a courtship employed by great numbers of plants. It is good to know of plants trysting in the wind; better still to see the beauty of the union.

Devoid of apparatus to attract pollinators, the flowers of grasses are simple and direct of purpose. Their sexual parts are clearly exposed and functionally explicit. As in all plants, the flowers of grasses are given special attention by scientists in assessing degrees of evolutionary advancement; those grasses with the most simple structures are termed *basic,* while those bearing more complex and specialized floral organs are said to be *advanced.* Grasses have some floral parts unique to their family, or at least known by specialized names. I will suggest several references offering precise botanical descriptions and spare you my own attempts. (A. S. Hitchcock's *Manual of the Grasses of the United States* is held to be authoritative. Agnes Chase's *First Book of Grasses* is more basic.) Descriptions I have read quickly deteriorate into a convolution of involucres, glumes, paleas, lemmas and other specialized grass parts from which I have never been able to gain a mental picture of a grass flower. Therefore I doubt I could paint one.

I offer instead some photographs and my interpretation of what can be seen with the flower in your hand.

It is August. Or April or October or any other relatively frost-free month. The grasses are in bloom. Along the sidewalk, against the trees and fenceposts and in a hundred hard-to-mow places, you see the tall, obvious shafts of crabgrass and Dallis grass

erect on vertical stems with horizontal branchlets decked in purple, red and blue. You pick one and hold it up to the light.

Tightly packed along the three-inch branches, the flowers hang from little stems. The dark anthers, the flowers' male parts, dangle on tiny threads and release a powder of pollen into the air. Tiny purple Christmas trees, like the gills of the stream eft, befrill the rachis. These are the stigmas on which the pollen grains alight and germinate.

Carefully separating one of the flowers from the cluster, you find that the exposed organs protrude from a green case which will nurture and shelter the developing seed. If we were looking at an insect-pollinated flower, the palea and lemma encasing the ovaries would perhaps be enlarged and differentiated into showy petals and bracts, enshrouding the external sexual parts as well as the ovaries, and, in a sense, obscuring their functions. But in its simplicity, the Dallis grass flower bares its external genitalia in direct association with the womb, passing the entire reproductive term, with minor changes, in a form easily identifiable as a developing seed. Later the stigmas and anthers will wither, the seed case will swell and turn brown, the palea and lemma will become the husks encasing the grain. But for now the stigmas curve from the seed case like the horns of a tiny lyre, the filaments of the anthers nothing more than strings for the wind to pluck.

Not a bad find for so humble a spot as the base of your gutter spout. You begin to look in the mowed part of the yard. Recalling that a week or two has passed since the last cutting, you notice the grass tops have taken on a purple cast. You squat and squint. Sure enough, the color comes from the crow-footed floral displays on the Bermuda grass blooming at your shoelaces. A closer inspection is a little more difficult than with the much taller Dallis grass, but, presbyopia permitting, you pick out a single flower with a knife point or tweezers. Again, the bare, green seed case has sprouted the little pencil points on tiny threads between the tiny feathers. The basic format is the same. And you find in time that other grasses in other lawns, and in limitless unlikely spots along your path, flower and fruit for all to see who will.

It comes to pass that on a day in May you drive past a growing field of wheat. The long, bearded heads have just formed and, recalling that wheat, too, is a grass, you stop by the roadside to see the breakfast of champions in bloom. Without leaving your car, you can see the half-inch yellow anthers vibrating in the breeze. Today, countless millions of pollen grains; three weeks hence, wheat germ for your salad.

The season being apt, you find other fields of small grain in bloom. Barley, with its short, fat heads; oats in flattened floral clusters; at the right moment, all display the filaments and feathers characteristic of their tribe. The shapes and sizes vary; the colors shift. You add the loveliness of each to your mental collection. And you fasten within you the enormous understanding that cereal doesn't come from boxes whose tops can be exchanged for trinkets. Like everything else involved in our care and feeding, the cereals have a life story uniquely theirs, but totally enmeshed with our own.

And the fuzzy-headed foxtail grass in the meadow—not really cultivated by people, but still a principal crop for the wintering sparrows. On a spring day you look between the fresh green bristles and find the floral colors. As the head turns gold in summer, then silver with frost, the foxtail grass is an old friend: you were present at its nuptials.

Pursuing life's mysteries, we always find that the plot thickens. Lawn grasses, canes and cereals are in the taxonomic midrange of the grass family, based on the complexity of their flowers. To me, though, they appear relatively simple in that the male and female parts sprout from the same structure which will ultimately house the seed. Other grasses have grown more complex.

Gamma grass shows the first evidence of separate quarters for the sexes. The first few nodes on the floral stem are definitely feminine; graceful pubescent stigmas an inch long curve sinuously from the rachis. The male flowers occupy the upper story, lowering the anthers from their sheaths at the proper moment to rain pollen on the ladies below—or better yet, on the ladies of the neighboring plants.

Gamma grass is common in the United States, but not plentiful. It grows head-high, with conspicuous flowers. It volunteers along roadsides and is sometimes cultivated as an ornamental. Inspecting gamma grass closely is an experience; you cannot but

117

The female flowers of gamma grass, marked by inch-long purple stigmas, are located separately above the male flowers.

see the differentiating forces of evolution at work in this rudimentary departure from the sexual arrangement of lawn grasses.

A Mexican grass, teosinte, takes the differentiation a step further. It separates the sexes entirely on separate stems located on different parts of the plant. Teosinte is not well established north of Mexico and we are unlikely to see it. I never have. But it is worth mentioning for its obvious link with the ultimate grass —*Zea mays.*

Corn.

The noted agrostologist (that's a grassologist) A. S. Hitchcock, had this to say about corn:

Maize or Indian Corn is one of the important economic plants of the world, being cultivated for food for man and domestic animals and for forage. It originated in America probably on the Mexican Plateau, and was cultivated from prehistoric times by the early races of American Aborigines, from Peru to middle North America. Several races of maize are grown in the United States, the most important being dent, the commercial field sort, flint, sweet, and pop.

Corn situates the male flowers at the crown of the plant in a branching arrangement commonly called the tassel. If you're a farmer, you have strong feelings about tassels. Their appearance signifies the end of growth. With inadequate rainfall the corn "tassels out" at a stunted three feet and puts all its energy into reproduction. In good seasons the tassels don't appear until the crowns are beyond a tall man's reach. Then the "silk" also begins to show at the tips of the cobs. Cornsilk is the stigmas of the female flowers which develop at leaf nodes along the stalk. Each floret along the corn's rachis (cob) sends its silk strand (style) upward to the opening at the top of the husks. Pollen grains alight on the silk and send an extension of their single cell down the full length of the style—sometimes over one foot. The ovary at the end of the silken style is then fertilized and the kernel begins to grow.

Ever husk an ear of corn and find a lot of the kernels stunted and undeveloped? I once planted several rows of corn in my garden a week apart hoping to have a continuous supply in late summer. The corn grew admirably but most of the kernels failed to develop. My dairy farmer neighbor had a ready explanation.

"Your corn had a poor sex life," he said.

I had planted the corn in rows across the wind and the pollen was blown away before it got to the silk. Several rows of the same age side by side would have enlivened the proceedings.

And so, I thought, how neatly it all fell into place—all these nuances of wind pollination. The simpler grasses cluster their tiny male and female parts together in a single flower as a safeguard (self-pollination) if cross-pollination fails. The more sophisticated grasses go to greater lengths to secure cross-pollination by enlarging and differentiating their flowers, forcing the pollen to travel greater distances. On the wings of the wind.

Then, as my eyes caressed the sunlit iridescence of the corn silk in my garden, I heard the hum of a tiny bee. She buzzed before my face to study the disruption of her territory (me), then went unerringly to the corn silk. There she probed and preened the glowing strands. Above my head there was more buzzing. A similar bee worked the dangling anthers, swinging like a trapeze artist from one to the next, nibbling and stroking each for a second or so.

Understanding faded once again into puzzlement. The bees conceivably (but improbably) could be on the flowers for some purpose other than gathering pollen. Nevertheless, they could not have avoided transporting the pollen if they had wanted to. I began to notice my corn patch more closely. Tiny flying insects were always on the flowers.

And the experts? Grass experts are no less human than you

and I. True, today they point out how clearly the grasses' floral structures imply wind pollination. But one day one of them will be lying in the grass, as we all must from time to time, watching the clouds make faces at him. And just possibly a little syrphid fly will alight on the Dallis grass spike next to his head and begin to dab at the flowers. His throat will go dry, though he dare not swallow and have his bobbing Adam's apple scare the fly.

Perhaps he will close his eyes and see a colleague standing before him in rumpled tweeds, waiting to be jabbed at with a pipe stem.

"Think of the implications!" he will demand of the colleague.

Then he will open his eyes and the syrphid will be gone. But on the top stem of the Dallis grass will be a tiny crab-spider, arms outstretched to embrace a pollinator.

"You knew, didn't you?" the agrostologist will say to the spider. "You knew all along."

Ignoring the botanical adage that grasses are totally wind-pollinated, a syrphid fly visits the flowers of dallis grass.

8 / *Caterpillars-In Their Own Right*

THERE IS A MYSTIQUE about caterpillars. It is best appreciated by small children and other dreamers but is beyond the ken of pragmatists. It has to do with the disturbing magic caterpillars exercise when, at the time of their choosing, they enshroud themselves in a chrysalid case and in its secrecy completely rearrange their cells to emerge transformed no less than Cinderella's pumpkin. The process suggests the medieval "spontaneous generation" concept, which had birds springing from falling leaves and animals from broken rocks. Today, casual observers and scientists alike find the transmutation of caterpillars into colorful moths and butterflies a preposterous alchemy.

It is true that, beneath the undulating fuzz, lurks the magic that will elevate the pedestrian caterpillar to the insect jet set. But the caterpillar's metamorphosis has been studied and photographed and written about extensively, with each work concluding that "further study" is necessary. So let us put this mystery aside for now.

Without the hocus-pocus, what have we left, just a dumb furry worm?

Au contraire.

Before reaching adulthood, caterpillars must run a deadly gauntlet. Their predators, parasites and pathogens are legion. The toll is frightful. But the caterpillars are not without resources. In their methods of coping, the caterpillars present limitless op-

121

portunities to observe life's processes and interactions. If you want something in nature to marvel at on a backyard safari, try caterpillars.

Caterpillars are the larval stages of moths and butterflies and skippers. They begin as eggs, usually laid in an open, unprotected cluster on vegetation. They grow in stages called instars. The skins are inelastic and must be shed periodically to permit growth. Some complete the entire larval experience in two or three weeks; others take all summer. A few overwinter as larvae, developed perhaps within the egg but unhatched, or hatched and partially grown in a wintering envelope of vegetation, a hibernaculum.

The caterpillar has been called "simply an eating machine," an apt description of its structure and its habits. Professor Klots describes the caterpillar as "the nutritive part of a butterfly's life cycle. Undisturbed by thoughts of sex or travel (in fact, undisturbed by thoughts) a larva eats, and eats, and then eats some more." The consumption of vast volumes of food is necessary to fuel the growth process, all of which occurs during the larval stage. Sufficient energy must also be stored to sustain the metamorphic struggle. The caterpillars of some moths must eat enough to nourish the adult stage as well, for the adults may not eat. They may even lack mouth parts.

Plant foliage is the principal food of caterpillars. Most species spend their days (though some wisely feed at night to avoid predators) chewing away at the leaves of their favorite plant. Some, like the monarch butterfly larvae, feed only on a single fodder, while others take a more varied diet. The mother makes food-finding easier for the hatchlings by laying her eggs on an edible plant. Typically, a caterpillar can choose between several related plants. The huge and fearsome royal walnut caterpillar, for example, can feast on hickory, sumac and sweet gum as well as its namesake tree. Some caterpillars have more catholic tastes and can be found on a wide variety of plants, chewing not only foliage but buds, fruits and seeds as well. One authority cites poison ivy as the one plant thought to escape the attentions of lepidopterous larvae.

But not all are herbivores. Sibling cannibalism is a reality

122

among some species. Perhaps a grim way to break up a family, cannibalism may be one of the forces which disperse young caterpillars, promoting access to new food supplies. The larva of one moth is known to be an internal parasite on other insects. And the caterpillar of one small butterfly, the harvester, common in eastern North America, is a true predator. It eats woolly aphids.

Some distinctive anatomical features unite all caterpillars. They lack the many-faceted compound eyes of the adults, but do retain a crescent of simple eyes (ocelli) on each side of the head. The lower half of the head is given over to the chewing mouth parts; the lower lip contains openings through which silk strands are extruded. True to insect character, caterpillars have six real legs, a pair on each of the first three body segments. The real legs are jointed, encased in chitinous shields and tipped with a single claw. Aft segments support two to five pairs of soft, leglike appendages called prolegs which terminate in pads lined with minute hooklets for clinging. The prolegs are shed with the skin in the final molt. A row of openings (spiracles) for the breathing passages ornament each side of the body.

Desmond Morris's naked ape isn't really naked. Our bodies are covered with tiny hairs which some would say are vestiges of a prehistoric pelage. Likewise, even the "naked" caterpillars have "hairs" (setae) on their bodies. These hairs serve a variety of protective functions, as we will see. They also provide a basis for taxonomic classification—if you happen to be an insect taxonomist armed with a microscope and a few thousand maps of the positions of the body hairs on various caterpillars. Each species has a special arrangement of hairs growing from tubercles on its skin. The patterns are basically common to a family, with unique variations of each species.

Short of this sort of tedious examination, I know of no reliable means of identifying caterpillars. Authorities hesitate even to offer guidelines for distinguishing the caterpillars of moths from those of butterflies, except for the generalization that moth larvae spin cocoons and butterfly larvae pupate in a thinner, more form-fitting envelope. But that information isn't particularly useful when you're looking at a caterpillar munching on a leaf. From my own experience I will cautiously offer a field distinction.

123

Body hairs grow from setiferous tubercles in unique patterns on each species of caterpillar providing a reliable, tedious, means of identification. This is a polyphemus moth larva.

Often, but by no means always, the fuzzy caterpillars are moth larvae while the "hairless" varieties, especially those with fleshy projections, will become butterflies. I'll put it another way. Page forty-nine of the Peterson Field Guide Series' *A Field Guide to the Butterflies* (by Alexander B. Klots) shows an assortment of butterfly larvae at various stages. None is hairy. A few have spiny projections. Other guides show the hairy types plus a good many bald caterpillars as being moth larvae. Among the hairless group, the chunky, fat ones tend to be moth larvae. Beyond these vague parameters I am lost.

Frankly, I like it better that way. Authorities estimate that only ten percent of the world's insects have so far been identified. So the ten thousand known species of moths, butterflies and skippers in North America may represent only a fraction of our total lepidopterous insects. The larvae of some change drastically in appearance from the early instars to the late. Faced with this seemingly endless larval variety, I have long since stopped trying to identify every caterpillar I find. Field guides are sometimes useful, but they are able to provide only a few examples from each family of Lepidoptera, with illustrations concentrating more on the adult forms than on the larval. But I find it exciting that I can step outside any summer day and find caterpillars I do not know. And maybe no one else knows them either.

There is much against which caterpillars must defend; up with which they must put. From thousands of miles to the south come the wood warblers, caterpillar-hungry. North come the thrushes and robins, the vireos and wrens. They've all got big families, and caterpillars head the grocery list. Snakes, lizards, shrews, wasps; they all eat caterpillars. Voraciously.

It's almost a little spooky to watch a paper wasp attack a caterpillar. The wasp buzzes up and down the willow leaves like a nearsighted Mr. Magoo, fondling every surface with vibrating antennae. Nearing a victim, the wasp becomes ecstatic. And erratic. The wings rev up to a screaming whine and the wasp gropes and gyrates wildly, tantalized by the scent. Then, contact! The wasp seizes its victim and begins to bite viciously, slashing open the caterpillar and letting the green blood spurt. Blood and plant juices the caterpillar has eaten, for the caterpillar, you re-

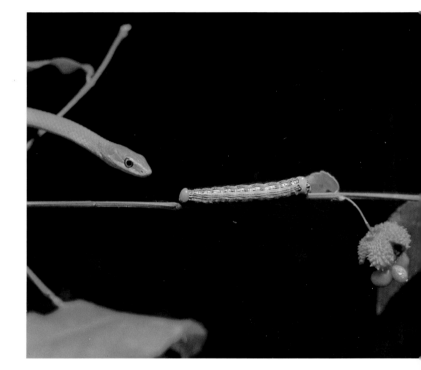

A rough green snake, one of many caterpillar predators, zeroes in on its prey on a strawberry bush.

member, is an eating machine—skin stretched over a stuffed digestive tract. The wasp dances and bites, buzzes and bites, chewing the caterpillar, sucking the juices. The killer whirls wildly, a frenzied blur of crazed lurches until, after some minutes, the inch-long worm that undulated with a strange grace is chewed to a blackened pea. The wasp flies off with its compacted prize. The eerie part is that the struggling forms may tumble over half a dozen other caterpillars too intent on munching willow to take notice.

And the fringillids who demurely cracked seeds at our feeders under the hibernal overcast—they, too, become predators. A cardinal picks a caterpillar off a leaf, hops to a limb and systematically beats it to a pulp. Into the gaping maw of a noisy nestling goes another caterpillar.

From the crowns of the oaks to the flowers of the Dallis grass the hunt goes on. What the mockingbird misses the green snake gets. What eludes the quick death of the paper wasp's slashing jaws feels the excruciatingly slow gnawing of the ichneumon's larvae burrowing into its body. Survival seems hopeless.

But it is a game of numbers—not entirely hopeless, just ninety-eight percent so. If one in fifty survives, or one in a thousand, what's the difference? say the caterpillars. One fat female butterfly cementing a cluster of eggs on the right plant this fall is all it takes to win. To keep the species in the game of life. The defensive extremes which the caterpillars employ testify to the murderous efficiency of the offense.

Earlier we mentioned the "hairs" (setae) on the caterpillar's bodies as a means of laboratory identification. On some species

The caterpillars are numberless, their predators legion. Here a paper wasp attacks a tent caterpillar, its green blood spurting where the killer's jaws have slashed.

the hairs have developed into clever, effective and sometimes fearsome protective devices. The shaggy plume moth larva becomes an unappetizing wad of fur. Stiff bristles make the tiger moth larva nearly impossible to pick up, probably more difficult still to swallow. The bristles on a few caterpillars have evolved into hypodermic needles for injecting painful irritants into a marauder's skin. I have the sharpest recollection of brushing my arm against a saddleback caterpillar while photographing the plant on which it fed. An intense pain swept over my arm; strangely, the only relief came from letting the limb hang limp at my side. The discomfort lasted for some minutes but left no aftereffects. Except that I am now as firmly "imprinted" with the need to avoid saddlebacks as any bird that ever let those bristles touch its soft palate.

By the time I met the royal walnut caterpillar I had a wholesome respect for modified setae, although previous experience would hardly have been necessary to suggest caution with this monster. To begin with, it is exactly the size of a hot dog. Two black eyespots frown from beneath a veritable set of antlers arching upward from the apparent crown of its head. I touched

Cocoons on the saddleback caterpillar, probably those of a braconid wasp, house ravenous larvae which feast upon the host, often killing it.

127

Antlered above false eye spots, the hotdog-sized royal walnut caterpillar represents an extreme in the development of protective body hairs.

the little green dragon with a stick and found that's the way the weapons are employed—as antlers. With violent lateral slashes the caterpillar thrust at the stick. These spines are not poison-tipped, but the mechanical damage the creature could do to a

128

human hand would, I suspect, be impressive. In this case, I avoided any empirical tests.

The specialized body hairs are not limited to weaponry and armor. For some they provide camouflage. For others they create the appearance of an object which would be of no interest to a predator, like a feather (that's one I have observed but have seen no reference to in my readings). Or a dandelion gone to seed. Or a mantis' egg clutch.

The defensive tactics are as plentiful as the species; and that, we have already noted, is a very large number. Some even change tactics as they grow. The hatchling and pupal stages of the spicebush swallowtail resemble quite different bird droppings while the maturing larva later wears a frightful mask painted on its upper thorax. When disturbed the larva rears the front half of its body up into a defiant stance and displays a fearsome visage. Aha! Mimicry, we say. Yet is this the proper term for the impersonation of a creature which never existed? Anyway, experiments have shown that eyespots so displayed are successful bird spookers. Over time, the pressures of bird predation bore less heavily on spicebush larvae who looked and behaved like a fearsome . . . something. Thus natural selection gave those with eyespots a chance to reproduce; gave those without the markings a one-way ticket down a bird's gullet.

The vaudevillians called it "doing a take"—the business of taking a stance in an exaggerated posture. For effect. Caterpillars are great doers of takes. Even among those without eyespots, some species do defensive takes when molested. Some curl into a tight ball and fall from the shrubbery foliage into, hopefully, the

Resembling an object of no interest to birds, such as their own droppings, is another means by which some caterpillars avoid predation.

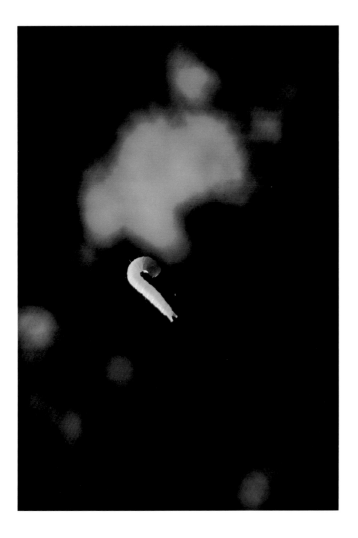

To escape attackers, some tree-dwelling caterpillars leap to safety from great heights, spinning a safety line as they fall. The climb back up can take hours.

protection of tall grass. Another grips with its middle prolegs and arches both ends gracefully upward in a frozen ballet stance. If that's not enough, it regurgitates a drop of green goo. Some with thorny projections release the grip of their front legs and dangle head down as if to bring the maximum number of spines to bear on an aggressor.

Coloration is a protective theme the caterpillars play masterfully. They use color in camouflage, and in object resemblance, of which you can find a dozen examples on any summer stroll. There is also a chromatic ruse called "flash and dazzle coloration." Some larvae, for example, flash a red collar momentarily when disturbed. They also protrude a red filament from each of two tubular projections on their tails suggesting the stylized flicker of a snake's tongue. A real show-stopper, this display gives pause even to the hungriest bird.

Birds, like all of us, inherit part of their lifestyle and learn the rest. Food selection is among the birds' learned behavior; each individual must learn by trial and error what is good and what noxious. Young birds learn very quickly. A single experience is usually enough to fix in mind whether a certain caterpillar is tasty or whether it is even food. If, for example, a bird somehow recognizes (usually by stepping on) a twig caterpillar as food, it will then begin to pick at twigs resembling twig caterpillars. After a few wasted gestures, the bird concludes that twigs are really twigs, and why bother.

The caterpillars capitalize in countless ways on the birds' swift learning ability. The monarch larva girdles itself with transverse stripes to clearly advertise its presence against the milkweed

130

leaves on which it feeds, gaining from the plant's chemistry an acrid taste. One attempt to swallow this foul-flavored creature permanently associates the black, white and yellow stripes with an instant desire to retch. Other caterpillars, even other creatures, bearing black and yellow colors reap the residual benefits. The mimicry apparently need not be precise; even a remote suggestion affords some benefit. The sequel to this tasteless tale is that the monarch's flavor continues in the adult even after its diet switches to nectar. Birds don't eat the adult either, so the adult viceroy butterfly copies the monarch's colors and flips about its business unmolested, yet perfectly edible. Bad taste, pain, object resemblance, all these devices rely on the birds' quick brains. If the caterpillars' predators were dull-witted, the high frequency of re-education (every textbook being another larva) would reduce the effectiveness of the defenses.

We know moths as creatures of the night. Many of their larvae employ this same means of avoiding birds and wasps. Some retire by day to individual redoubts often fashioned by rolling together the sides of a living leaf and weaving themselves into a tightly shut mantle. The more gregarious caterpillars hole up during daylight in large communal tents, woven by a group effort of lower-lip silk glands. I know of no instance of birds tearing open a tent defense. However, I have opened webs in trees in my orchard and watched mockingbirds gorge themselves on the caterpillars. And once I watched a wasp struggle across one of these multilayered tents, seemingly addled by the delicious smells within. At times the wasp appeared to be caught in the webbing it was trying to penetrate. Tediously the wasp circled the web, its claws tearing at the threads. Several caterpillars ventured near the outer layer to repair the damage. And again I witnessed the paroxysms of joy produced in the wasp by caterpillar juices.

To me, caterpillar watching represents an important medium of experience—that of selecting a theme and catching its variations. It is hard to see a caterpillar without musing on the similarity of its spines to those on one you saw last week and without, as a consequence, wondering how they are related. Harder still to suppress the questions posed by two obviously unrelated species with a similar defense. Nature bombards our senses daily with

131

countless random impressions. We can absorb only so much. Plus a little more when the material is related to previous experience.

So we pick a theme or two to pursue this season. Caterpillars are good. But it could have been spiders (any creature whose adaptations include no less a trick than flying without wings has to be worth spending some time with). Or perhaps the solitary wasps, those harmless (to man) and totally fascinating hawks of the insect realm. Spiders, wasps, bats, beetles, caterpillars, whatever. It is a question of what is available, what waylays your fancy between the front door and the sidewalk. We shuffle this season's themes around on the burners of our stove of inquiry with those of other seasons. The themes eventually simmer into a *weltanschauung* uniquely suited to our taste; into a very delicious, very personal interpretation of life.

9 / *The Ecosystem in My House*

HOME. Midmorning. Early June. Hours ago the crepuscular debate of barred owls and whippoorwills stirred our sleep, curled us into a single fetal figure. Now we lie abed late, replete with love and sleep. The windows stand open, admitting a gentle bath of air at exactly the right temperature, at once warming and cooling. And the light . . . so clean and fresh streaming into the little sleeping loft, bearing some of the new greens from the young foliage outside the window. A cuckoo *ga-loops* softly on the breeze. And scattered lines from a Housman poem ("Bredon Hill") I was obliged to memorize in high school, and thought to be long forgotten, *ga-loop* gently through my mind:

> *Here on a Sunday morning*
> *My love and I would lie;*
> *And see the colored counties,*
> *And hear the larks so high . . .*

Splat! Drip. Drip.

I sit bolt upright in bed. A milky mess drips from the dresser top into the open drawer containing my socks. Approaching the dresser, I note with deepening chagrin that there is also some solid matter. The mixture looks distressingly like fecal material. But where . . . ? Such things come only from above. I look toward the ceiling. Through an unfinished joint in the sheetrock, I watch the last few inches of a black rat snake glide casually across the gap.

133

How's that for openers? A snake using my snug little bedroom for a latrine. Shocking? I found it so and I quickly resolved to plaster up the hole. And all others like it. My cabin in the country is old, you see, with walls and rafters hewn from white oak logs. It is free of straight lines, of plumb surfaces. Nothing fits right in the carpentry by which I attempted to seal out the cold endured by earlier occupants. The rough-hewn structure seems intent on rejecting the insulation and sheetrock wallboard. Crevices gape everywhere waiting to be plastered over, serving meanwhile as avenues of ingress and egress for air and animals.

I would address the joints with tape and plaster. But about the snake I would do nothing. Couldn't if I wanted to. Not without dismantling the house log by log. Anyway, my mind had long since been made up about the snake. It was a necessary ally, and I wasn't going to let a brief lapse in personal hygiene change our relationship.

We like to think of ourselves as masters and sole occupants of our homes. Forget it. In spite of the best efforts of the most meticulous housewife, in spite of the boniest finger of the most officious FHA inspector pointed at the inadequately treated underpinnings, in spite of the hardest marketing drives of manufacturers of the most lethal household pesticides, a horde of nonhumans precedes the two-legged occupants into every house and stays there long after the human inhabitants have gone.

This discussion may, if it hasn't already, become a bit direct for the fastidious. We may as well break the ice. If we find it difficult to handle the thought of sharing shelter with other organisms, let us first fathom that we are not even sole occupants of our own bodies. Depending on a great many factors frequently independent of our futile splashings at personal cleanliness, the human body hosts numberless plant and animal parasites. Any medical text on human parasitology will catalogue endless animals who crawl, suck, chew and flagellate their way over and through us. The plant kingdom, represented by the fungi, finds the human carcass a veritable greenhouse. We are usually unaware of the way these "lower" life forms use us until some sort of lesion results. Even then we find it more comfortable to think of the problem as an illness or an injury rather than as a parasitic infec-

134

tion. Yet for all our public health programs, our sex education and our hideously expensive medical services, the human—yes, American—body swarms with macro- and microorganisms which generally stay in a state of dynamic equilibrium with our protective mechanisms. To add a note of cheer, some of our microbes are helpful, even necessary to our vital functions.

So, too, are some of the creatures with whom we dwell. Oddly, they are the ones we typically fear most—the spider, the snake, the wasp. In short, the predators. Household predators carry a profound message which we obtusely refuse to heed. They wouldn't be in our homes if there weren't prey there for them

A black rat snake, hopefully the most formidable predator commonly sharing human dwellings, tests the air for mouse scent.

to eat. The first law (don't ask me whose) of predation is that predators follow prey.

It is the prey, of course, who are the pernicious guests. Silverfish, cockroaches, fleas, flies, mice, rats, moths. Each householder can recite his own list of losses to these tireless despoilers whose business it is to ferret out the good, the important, the precious, and then to wreck them. I earnestly hope my tax return for 1969 is never audited, since some mouse, overcome with a matronly need for nesting material, chewed to shreds my bank statements for that year. But when the IRS auditor finally does come, I know he'll rejoice with me at the skin my resident black rat snake shed above one of the livingroom windows after growing fat on housemouse.

Whereas I can only hope the predators in my body have the prey in check, in my house I am confident of it. The place is not overrun with mice, but they are in evidence. Once, late at night,

135

I was awakened by the screams of a mouse suffocating in the maw of a snake (this time back in the attic). The next day a search yielded four snake skins in the attic, each neatly following the contours of a box or trunk. The skins all appeared to be deposited at different times, and the size seemed to increase slightly as the age of deposit grew more recent. The same snake, I guessed, cast them all, growing rapidly on attic mammals. So it seems to have gone, over the past few years—one or two black rat snakes in the house controlling a few dozen mice.

This conclusion brings us to the second law of predation. Briefly stated, it is that predators control, but do not eliminate the prey. As prey availability decreases, predators get hungry and go elsewhere. Or stay and starve. The prey get a chance to fill their decimated ranks, and before long the predators are back. The rule applies as well within human habitations as without.

What that means is that if you have mice and roaches now you probably always will. You'll just have to hope you also have enough rat snakes and spiders to control them.

Not so, you say? You can hire a man to come and "exterminate" your house? Let's talk about that a minute. The prey usually have shorter life cycles and more numerous offspring than the predators. Therefore the prey have much greater opportunity for genetic mutation than do the predators. They can respond more readily to the pesticide threat and therefore have a higher probability of developing resistant strains. And then you are in trouble. The wonderful poisons have killed off the natural controls and left you with a houseful of pesticide-resistant roaches. The exterminator, whom you've fired for his incompetence, is off extending his services to others who would rather live with poisons than with a few harmless expressions of the natural world.

It stretches a point to speak of a complete ecosystem within a house. Complete systems involve an interplay between primary producers and consumers of varying ordinal rank. The primary producers, or autotrophs, are the green plants and bacteria capable of making their own food. There are few if any primary producers active in our homes. The roof, after all, blocks the sunlight necessary for photosynthesis. Most of the energy which circulates between the walls and in the attic and basement comes

136

from without. That is, it comes from outdoor autotrophs. Some enters the house in the bodies of insects and vertebrates, there to be consumed by higher organisms. But much of the sustaining force arrives in the shopping bags of the human occupants. All to the delight of a legion of consumers — heterotrophs like ourselves — who derive nourishment from organic matter.

Welcome, then, to my modest dwelling, this house of heterotrophs. Tea? No? Sherry? Good. Tell me of your trip. Rest here awhile. We will talk and enjoy a visit with the other guests.

That mantis on the curtain by your head, for example. I love mantises. Sometimes when I'm out walking, I'll perch one on my finger, then let it climb up my sleeve and ride on my shoulder. This mantis went the extra mile with me. I didn't realize he was still on my shirt until he jumped for the curtain when I sat down. He spends his days now catching flies on the window, creeping up on them between the folds in the material. The flies are attracted to the light and the mantis knows it. He swivels his head around and follows them as they buzz and bump against the glass. When one comes within range, it's all over more quickly than the eye can follow. One instant the fly is in flight; the next the mantis is serenely chewing off its head. I'll have to remember to take this chap to the garden soon. And maybe invite another in to de-fly the window.

That funnel-shaped web bracketing the right angle between the wall and the kitchen counter is the work of an Agelenid spider. There is a cosmopolitan niece in this family known as the European house spider, which this might well be. *Tegenaria domestica,*

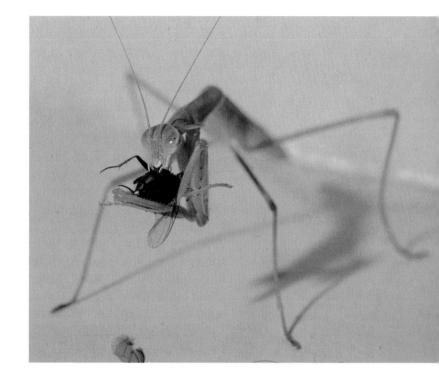

A praying mantis lives handsomely on flies caught flying at the windowpanes.

137

if you please, upon first introduction. She's shy, but friendly and easy to get to know. She lives in houses the world over because she likes the flies and roaches we draw. Let's see if she's hungry. There's always a roach or two in the cabinet under the sink. Here we go. Oops! Roaches are hard to catch without squashing. Still kicking, though. Now suppose a roach crossed the kitchen counter foraging for crumbs, came to the wall, turned left and climbed down the side. Like so. Just about the time the roach's antennae tickle the flat shelf of the Agelenid's web, she explodes from the tunnel opening, like a charge from the muzzle of a shotgun.

If you'll look closely at the lower left corner of the lower right glass pane in the kitchen door, you'll see another shelf-and-funnel web. Tiny, isn't it. The whole web is hardly an inch long. A strapping housefly is too much for that little Agelenid. I've seen them shred her web and escape. But, she likes mosquitoes—she, and her spouse, who discreetly occupies the underside of the shelf web, feeding on her kills from beneath. As in many spider species, the female is larger than the male and, except at "special" times, regards him as nothing more than a handy protein source. So the male keeps his distance, approaching only after strumming the web with his tranquilizing love song.

The big orb-weavers don't do very well in houses. One reason that comes to mind is that their webs, to be effective, must span the major throughways of flying insects. That means hallways, doorways and staircases, which also happen to be human thoroughfares. The webs are large and anything but unobtrusive. I'll admit to being an indifferent housekeeper, but pulling orb-webs out of my face on the way to the bathroom at night is a bit much even for me.

But I'll show you a different web I'll bet you can find in your house. It's commonly called the cobweb; that irregular, three-dimensional grid of minute threads that is usually visible only when outlined in collected dust. Cobwebs summon a certain reality avoidance from somewhere in our troubled dreams. We know inwardly that cobwebs are evidence of animals. But we prefer to see them as detached units of untidiness of vague origin rather than as the capturing nets of tiny killers at large in our homes. The fact is, cobwebs are the work of spiders in the family

138

Wolf spiders spin no webs, but like wolves, take their prey in fair chase. They are adept at pursuing roaches and silverfish in the crevices of human habitations. This mother carries her egg clutch and newly-hatched brood.

Theridiidae, the comb-footed spiders, and often of the very common American house spider, a family member who should be welcome at least in the less formal parts of any home. When dust

makes the webs offensive, you can take them down with a broom. If you're careful to let the house spider escape, she will rebuild the web in a few hours with clean silk. The only care and maintenance necessary will then be occasionally to sweep up the little collection of leftovers from beneath the web.

Have you ever seen a house spider make a capture? They can handle prey many times their size and strength by repeatedly lassoing the victim with silk. The comb on the fourth leg plays out the silk, wrapping the captive in a fine swaddle. The stronger the prey, the more frantically the house spider throws her silken loops. Gradually the victim tires, the spider inches ahead in the race to spin new bonds before the old are broken. The thrashing slows; the fetters tighten. Shackled, the victim is bitten and drained.

Here on the porch is my favorite roach and silverfish artist, the wolf spider. I am so glad you could meet. If you object to any of the spiders you just saw because of the webs they leave around the house, you'll have to find another protest for the wolf spider. She spins not, except for the silken egg case she's carrying. But toil she does—mothering her brood and taking her prey on the run. Her way is to pursue the crawling insects into their hiding places, a capital adaptation for ferreting camel crickets and roaches out of the woodwork. Her young will stay with her until their first molt; a week or two. I once accidentally bumped a mother wolf spider, pummeling her over and unseating half her brood. She stood her ground while the spiderlings scurried up her legs. With a wave of her pedipalps she wiped the last of the minute mahouts out of her eyes and hastened for cover.

Enough spiders for one day? I agree. Just enough to keep the household insects in check. I can't blame you for wanting to meet some creatures who don't have quite so many eyes and legs. We've got lots more mammals, all cute and furry. If you'll stay the night you'll probably hear the flying squirrels playing in the attic. They're nocturnal, with eyes that glow like coals when you catch them in the beam of a flashlight. Some gray squirrels also live in the attic. Aside from differences in size and in aerodynamic qualities, the way we tell them apart around this house is that the flying squirrels keep you awake taking laps above the ceiling at

140

night, while the gray squirrels keep you awake if you're trying to take an afternoon nap.

We've got bats, too. They sleep in the attic during the day, but sometimes one finds its way downstairs and has to be let out at sundown. I've really got to get to work on that sheetrock. I avoid handling bats because of some things I've read about rabies, but they're probably harmless. Except that it doesn't take too many bats too long to enrich your attic-stored belongings with a stratum of guano. But organic enrichment is one of the expected results of occupancy by animals. All of us do it. I just hope the rat snake doesn't take it upon himself to enrich my socks again.

Bats frequently roost in attics. This little brown bat occasionally came downstairs on its way out of my house, requiring assistance at the door.

We haven't heard from all the rodents yet. Hispid cotton rats are common in the grass around the house. Some venture under the foundation and up between the log walls. Like the mice, and I suppose an occasional bat and flying squirrel, cotton rats probably contribute to the rat snake's welfare.

I have a weakness for lentil soup. The kind you make with real lentils and black-eyed peas and diced hot-dogs and onions. The mice, or whatever, have a weakness for elaborate practical jokes. Last winter I bought a pound bag of lentils, enough for a great vat of steaming, tasty soup. A few days later I opened the cupboard and the bag was empty. Muttering a dark oath of vengeance, I made do with a sandwich. I could be consoled and refreshed only by a hike in the woods, so I put on my woolly socks and pulled on my right boot. Then I jammed my foot into my left boot. And into a pound of lentils.

The route from the cupboard to the upstairs bedroom closet,

141

Under the porch eaves a Carolina wren feeds her young in a hanging planter, blurring the boundaries of human and wildlife habitat.

if you're three inches long and furtively carrying a cheekful of lentils, probably goes something like this: down the wall behind the cabinet, through the hole in the floor next to the sink drain, then under the house twenty feet, up the foundation and between

142

the log walls, up to the second floor, through another place where two pieces of sheetrock almost meet, and finally into the closet. I say it takes a highly developed sense of humor to sustain a few dozen or a few hundred trips along that route. Unfortunately, I didn't think it was at all funny.

There's something else in the attic. I don't know what it is. I only know what it says. *Boop—oop-oop-oop-oop.* Softly, late at night, when everything else is quiet. *Boop—oop, oop, oop, oop.* The last few oops percolate inquisitively upward, asking, sort of, who I am and if I know what *it* is. I never know how to respond. But you'll hear it tonight.

You won't be staying? Oh, I'm sorry. Such a short visit.

Oh, well. I'll just get myself a Pepsi and sit here on the back porch for a while. Alone. Ha! That's a laugh, being alone in this house. The porch is nice in the late afternoon. I mean, the way it provides a transition zone between the house and the outdoors, so that my world gently intergrades with theirs. Hi there, skink, sunning yourself on the steps. I'll bet you've been out on the bull-thistle in the yard. You're glad I haven't cut the grass yet this year, aren't you? Well, I just might not. Go ahead under the porch and get a wolf spider. Or maybe a few camel crickets along the foundation.

The phoebe makes a feeding visit to her nest beneath the porch eaves . . . I have to stop rocking while she's delivering flies or she'll make rude gestures at me with her tail from her perch on the grapevine. But the Carolina wren requires no deferential hush for her feeding visit. She'll feed her brood in the hanging planter while I'm taking a big pull on my Pepsi. Then pick a caterpillar off the porch post and beat it against the arm of the next chair. A mud dauber wasp pitches to her rack of organ pipes on the siding, to the one pipe that's still dark and damp. With her jaws buzzing in high C, she smooths her mudball cargo onto the chimney, adding an eighth of an inch to one side of the structure. Tomorrow she'll catch an Araneus, maybe from the web against the side of the house.

Yes, the porch. . . . How well it provides a transition from my world into theirs. But that's a laugh, too, isn't it. It's all their world. And mine, if I want to take a closer look.

143

Selected Index

Adder's tongue. See Lily, trout
Alder, 15, 36, 37, 47
    tag, 51, 72
Alfalfa, 111
Alga, 63
Anemone quinquefolia.
    See Wood anemone
Aphid, 7
Argiopidae. See Spiders, writing
Assassin bug, 12, 88
Aster, 45, 68
Avalanche lily. See Lily, avalanche
Bamboo, 111
Barley, 117
Barred owl. See Owl, barred
Bat, 141
Bee fly, 56
Beech drops, 72
Beetles
    bark, 86
    borer, 86
    long-horned, 85, 86
    Passalus, 85-87
    sawyer, 85, 86
    stag, 86
Beggar's lice, 46
Bermuda grass, 116
Black-capped chickadee.
    See Chickadee, black-capped
Black rat snake. See Rat snake, black
Blackfly, larva, 32
Blackberry, 45, 68, 99
Bleeding heart, 54

Bloodroot, 57
Bluebird, eastern, 80
Bluejay, 3, 4, 69, 98, 105, 107
Brassicaceae, 50
British Soldiers, 64
Butterflies
    hairstreak, 8
    harvester, 123
    monarch, 8, 45, 68, 122, 130-131
    painted lady, 8
    sulfur, 8
    tiger swallowtail, 8
    viceroy, 131
Broomsedge, 68, 70
Bug, true, 18
Bullbat, 45, 93
Bumblebee, 8, 10
Caddisfly, 23, 24, 25
    larva, 27, 28, 32
    nymph, 27
Camel cricket. See Cricket, camel
Cardinal, 47, 68, 94, 96, 98, 101, 105, 125
Cardinal flower, 36
Carolina Wren. See Wren, Carolina
Caterpillars, 121-132
    harvester butterfly larva, 123
    monarch butterfly larva, 45, 122, 130
    plume moth larva, 127
    royal walnut, 122, 127
    saddleback, 127
    spicebush swallowtail larva, 129
    tent, 131
    tiger moth larva, 127

Cedar, 46, 68, 69
    eastern red, 68
Cedar waxwing, 97, 99, 100
Chestnut, 50, 66, 73
Chickadee, black-capped, 80
Chickweed, 57
Chimney swift, 45
Chrysognomum, 72
Chub, 32, 33
Cicada, 7, 34
Cat, house, 108
Clam, 32, 39
    freshwater, 30, 31
    larva, 27, 31
Claytonia
    caroliniana. See Spring beauty
    lanceolata. See Spring beauty
    virginica. See Spring beauty
Clickbeetle, 7
Climax vegetation, 64-65
Clover, 111
Cobweb, 138, 140. See also Spiders,
    comb-footed
Cockleburr, 46
Cooper's hawk. See Hawk, Cooper's
Cordiceps, 88
Corn, 74, 111, 118, 119
Corydalis, 54
    golden, 54
Corydalis aurea. See Corydalis, golden
Corydalis sempervirens, 54
Crabgrass, 68
Crawfish, 31-34, 38
Crested flycatcher, 80
Cricket, camel, 140, 143
Dace, 32
Dallis grass, 114, 116, 120, 125
Damselfly, larva, 29, 32
Darter, 29, 30, 32
Decapod, 31,32
Dentaria laciniata. See Toothwort
Dicentra, 54
Dicentra eximia. See Bleeding Heart
Dobsonfly, larva, 29, 32
Dogtooth violet. See Lily, trout
Dragonfly, 45, 51
    larva, 32
    naiad, 29
    nymph, 30
Dutchman's breeches, 54

Eft, 22, 25, 32, 33, 116
Ephemeroptera, 27
Erythronium
    americum. See Lily, trout
    grandiflorum. See Lily, glacier
    montanum. See Lily, avalanche
Evening grosbeak.
    See Grosbeak, evening
False foxglove, 72
False rue anemone, 56
Firefly, 45, 67
Flying squirrel. See Squirrel, flying
Fox, gray, 46
Fox sparrow. See Sparrow, fox
Foxtail grass, 68, 117
Fringillidae, 47, 98
Fumariaceae, 50, 54
Fungus, 63, 83, 84-85, 87, 88
Funnel web, 137, 138. See also,
    Spiders, Agelnid
Gamma grass, 117
Glacier lily. See Lily, glacier
Golden corydalis.
    See Corydalis, golden
Goldfinch, 13, 45, 96, 104
    American, 70
Grasshopper, 7, 45
Gray fox. See Fox, gray
Green heron, 37
Grosbeak, evening, 70, 94, 97, 98,
    105, 108
Hairstreak butterfly. See Butterflies,
    hairstreak
Harvester butterfly. See Butterflies,
    harvester
Hawk
    Cooper's, 72, 73, 76
    Red-shouldered, 76
    Sharp-shinned, 73, 103, 108
Hellgrammite, 29, 88
Hemiptera. See Bug, true
Hepatica, 58, 72
Hispid cotton rat.
    See Rat, hispid cotton
Horned owl. See Owl, horned
Horseweed, 68
House cat. See Cat, house
Hummingbird, ruby-throated, 8, 10, 14,
    15, 36, 93, 100
Hydra, larva, 32

Isopyrun biternatum. See False rue
    anemone
Jack-in-the-pulpit, 57
Junco, 47, 68, 94, 98, 104, 108, 109.
    See also Snowbird
Junco hiemalis. See Junco.
Juniperus virginiana. See Cedar,
    eastern red.
Kingfisher, 10, 36, 37
Kinglet
    golden-crowned, 73, 94
    ruby-crowned, 73, 100, 101, 107
Leech, 22, 32
Lepidoptera, 124
Lespedeza, 111
Lichen, 62-64
Liliaceae, 50
Lily
    avalanche, 52
    glacier, 52
    trout, 50-56
Linyphiidae. See Spiders, linyphiid
Long-horned beetle. See Beetles, long-
    horned
Mantis, 12, 13, 137
    Carolina, 13
Marijuana, 111
Mayapple, 57
Mayfly, 23-27
    larva, 32
    naiad, 17
    nymph, 25, 29, 30
Maypop, 45
Meadowlark, 68
Merganser, 76
Millipede, 87
Mink, 39
Minnow, 30, 32, 37
Mockingbird, 43, 45, 96, 99, 100, 101,
    125, 131
Monarch butterfly. See Butterflies,
    monarch
Mud dauber wasp. See wasp, mud
    dauber
Mulberry, 72
Narrow-mouthed toad, 91
Nighthawk. See Bullbat
Oats. 111, 117
Opposum, North American, 40-41, 76
Oryza sativa. See Rice.

Owl
    barred, 38, 45, 69, 133
    horned, 43, 45, 47, 72, 76, 77, 82
    screech, 45
Painted lady butterfly. See Butterflies,
    painted lady
Paper wasp. See Wasp, paper
Passalus. See Beetles, Passalus
Passion flower. See Maypop
Phoebe, 43
    eastern, 100
Phytoplankton, 61
Piciforms, 79. See also Woodpecker
Pine, 59, 68-75, 82, 85, 94, 101
    long-leaf, 81
Plantain, 68
Poaceae, 110, 111
Poke, 46, 68, 98, 99
Portulacaceae, 50
Primrose, evening, 45
Purple finch, 70, 94, 96, 103, 104
Queen Anne's lace, 67
Raccoon, 15, 32, 39, 40, 76, 81, 90
Ranunculaceae, 50
Rat, hispid cotton, 141
Rat snake, black, 68, 133, 135, 136
Red-shouldered hawk. See Hawk, red-
    shouldered
Rice, 111
Rye, 111
Robber fly, 12
Royal walnut caterpillar. See
    Caterpillars, royal walnut
Salamander, 22, 38, 90
Sassafras, 72
Sawyer beetle. See Beetles, sawyer
Screech owl. See Owl, screech
Sharp-shinned hawk. See Hawk,
    sharp-shinned
Shiner, 32
Silphium, 65
Skink, five-lined, 3-6, 12, 143
Slime mold, 85, 87
Snail, 7, 21, 32, 87
    aquatic, 20
    shell, 41
Snapping turtle, 38
Snowbird, 47. See also Junco
Solomon's seal
    false, 72

true, 72
Sorghum, 111
Sorrel, 68
Spanish needle, 46
Sparrow
    fox, 105
    white-throated, 68, 94, 109
Spicebush, 47, 72
Spiders
    Agelnid, 137-138
    comb-footed, 139-140
    crab, 12, 120
    jumping, 12
    orb-web, 138
    water, 20
    wolf, 140, 143
    writing, 12
Sponge, 32
    fresh-water, 28
Spring beauty, 52-56
Squirrel corn, 54, 56
Squirrel, 46
    eastern gray, 140
    flying, 81, 140, 141
Stonefly, 23-25, 30, 34
    larva, 32
    nymph, 24-25, 30
Strawberry bush, 46, 99
Subimago, 27. See also Mayfly
Sugarcane, 111
Sulfur butterfly. See Butterflies, sulfur
Swallowtail, tiger, 8
Sweet gum, 69, 70, 72, 122
Syrphid fly, 12, 120
Tag alder. See Alder, tag
Tegenaria domestica. See Spiders,
    Agelnid
Teosinte, 118
Tent caterpillar. See Caterpillars, tent
Termite, 84, 87
Terrapin, 38
Theridiidae. See Spiders, comb-footed
Thomisidae. See Spiders, crab
Titmouse, 96, 98, 102, 104, 107
    tufted, 103
Towhee, rufous-sided, 47, 68, 94, 96,
    98, 104
Treehopper, 7
Trillium, 58
Twig caterpillar. See Caterpillars, twig

Toothwort, 56
Touch-me-not, spotted, 15, 34, 36
Trout lily. See Lily, trout
Tulip poplar, 54, 66, 70, 72, 76, 78
Vaccinium, 72
Viburnum, 72, 99
Viceroy butterfly. See Butterflies,
    viceroy
Warblers, 6, 73, 93, 101
Wasp
    mud dauber, 143
    paper, 125, 126
Water cycle, 17
Water penny, 29, 32
Watersnake, 22, 38
Waterstrider, 15, 18-20, 32
Water thrush, Louisiana, 37
Wheat, 11, 116, 117
Whippoorwill, 44, 93
Whirligig, 19, 20, 32
White-breasted nuthatch, 80, 102, 107
White-throated sparrow. See
    Sparrow, white-throated
Whooping crane, 44
Wild ginger, 72
Windflower, 57
Winter wren. See Wren, winter
Wintergreen, 72
Wood anemone, 53-54
Woodcock, 44, 47, 76
Wood duck, 76
Wood louse, 87
Woodpecker
    downy, 69, 76, 79, 101-102, 107
    pileated, 73, 76, 79, 80
    red-bellied, 76, 79, 107, 108
    red-cockaded, 81, 82
    red-headed, 73, 76, 101
Wooly mullein, 68
Worm snake, 90
Wren
    Carolina, 80, 99, 101, 143
    Winter, 93, 94
Yellow-shafted flicker, 73, 79
Zea mays. See Corn